Vaudeville Wit

LATEST
CROSS FIRE
JOKES

ILLUSTRATED

VAUDEVILLE
WIT

LATEST CROSS-FIRE CONVERSATIONS, GAGS,
REPARTEE, RETORTS AND MONOLOGUES FROM
THE AMERICAN VAUDEVILLE STAGE

With 75 Cartoons by Hall

Gathered by

CARLETON B. CASE

SHREWESBURY PUBLISHING CO.
CHICAGO

This facsimile reprint includes negative depictions and/or mistreatment of people or cultures. These stereotypes were wrong then and are wrong now.

Rather than remove this content, we want to acknowledge its harmful impact, learn from it and spark conversation to create a more inclusive future together.

VAUDEVILLE WIT

CHARLES BENSA AND FLORENCE BAIRD

"How do you like my figure?"

"Did you call that a figure?"

"No, it's merely a matter of form."

"I see that you're Scotch, and I suppose you play golf. What is your favorite course?"

"Soup."

"I don't mean that kind of a course. I mean what is your favorite links?"

"Sausage."

"Why is a Ford like a schoolroom?"

"What's the reason?"

"Both full of nuts with a crank at the head."

JACK WILSON AND COMPANY

"Did you see those classic dancers that just came ahead of us on the bill?"

"I certainly did. What are you mopping your brow for?"

"I'm warm. Those dancers did it. It seemed to me every time they danced they got rid of more clothes."

"Well, they've stopped now."

"Yes; I was sorry to see it happen, too."

"Did you notice that Hawaiian dance?"

"Yes, sir. All they wear down there is some baled hay. And if I ever get a vacation, Hawaii's the place I'm going to spend it."

"I hope you saw the girl with the million dollar eyes."

"She was lovely. She was a pippin. Such a figure!"

"Did you notice her eyes?"

"No, I wasn't looking at her eyes."

———

"I dined at ———'s last night."

"That's the place they steal your hat and coat, isn't it?"

"Yes."

"But you can always buy them back cheap."

"The food's great."

"Yes. Three split peas and a cracked plate— $2.80!"

EDDIE FOY AND SIX LITTLE FOYS

"Hello, Central. Gimme 1007456789543 New Rochelle. Nobody home? Whaddayamean nobody home? My family couldn't all go out at the same time.

"Hello. Yes. This is papa. Tell mamma I won't be home for dinner. What? She says it will be all right if I bring you home a doll. Well, what kind of a doll do you want? What? Your mother says to tell me I'll know what kind—that I know all about dolls. Well, you tell her I know enough not to bring the kind I know about home.

"Hello, son. How's things in New Rochelle? Say, son, which one is this? O, yes. Hello, kid. Load the folks into the car and come on downtown. Which car? Quit kidding; you know we only got one car—the truck. Get out of New Rochelle for the evening— that's the only town Columbus refused to discover.

"Hello. Who's this? O, you. What? The black chicken laid a duck egg today. Well, don't let the rooster know anything about it."

MARIE NORDSTROM
In "Twenty Years From Now."

"So you wish a position as a stenographer, young man?"

"Yes, m'am."

"How old are you?"

"I'm twenty-six, m'am."

"You're a good looking boy."

"Yes, m'am."

"Have you ever worked before?"

"Yes, m'am, at Mrs. McArthur's office."

"Were you discharged?"

"No, m'am."

"Then why did you quit?"

"I—I—was forced to leave, m'am."

"For what reason?"

"I—I'd rather not state."

"Did Mrs. McArthur make love to you?"

"Yes. But I'm not a bad man, m'am. I had to leave."

"Very well. You may go to work here. Hang up your hat."

"Yes, m'am."

"Now as to your duties: Frequently you will have

to stay downtown to work late, and in that ease you will take dinner with me."

"Oh, I beg you, m'am, to be as lenient as possible. I always go home to dinner. I'm father's sole support."

"Nevertheless you may have to work late sometimes. Perhaps till 10, then we can go out and have a spin in my car and a little drink."

"O, I couldn't do that, m'am. Father doesn't like to have me running around with strange women."

TOM LEWIS AND COMPANY

"Are you a pessimist?"

"No, I'm a Baptist."

"Were your forefathers all Mexicans?"

"I didn't have fourfathers. I only had one."

"You have an awful cold, haven't you?"

"Yes, I have."

"What are you doing for it?"

"Coughing."

"Speaking of Mexicans reminds me of the old adage, 'When Greek meets Greek—'"

"They open a restaurant."

HOLDEN AND HARRON

"They tell me you've been traveling."

"Yes, I've been on a tour."

"O, you've been on a tear."

"Not a tear; a tour. I went through Europe."

"Did you get many pocketbooks?"

"Certainly not. I went to Europe for my liver."

"Did you have a stormy trip?"

"Very."

"Seasick?"

"No, the sea wasn't; I was."

LEW FIELDS

Fields appears at the costume ball in a suit of tight-fitting red clothes and red top-hat.

"I feel like a bottle of tomatto catsup.

"The feller that sold me this costume told me these pants were satin. By golly, I don't know who sat-in 'em. I can't."

His wife appears in a long-trained gown cut very low in the back.

"My dear, that dress is too extreme for a respectable woman to wear. If the soldiers were exposed as much on the front as you are exposed on the back the war would be over. Go and get another dress."

"This dress is all right. It was made direct from the fashion plate. It is just like the plate."

"Then that plate was over-exposed."

" Believe me, Maria, you'll keep trying to break into society and pulling off one swell function after another, until you won't have anything left to pull off."

"Well, I'm going straight ahead with my plans, I don't care what comes off." She walks forward. Fields steps on her train and about ten yards of her costume drops to the floor.

" By golly, the whole verandah came off."

———

The tailor who made the wife's dress picks up the part she has left behind and says in exasperation:

" Oh, zee bootiful creation, it is ruined. If your wife must be so careless, she ought not to wear clothes at all."

" It's coming to that," says Fields, " it's coming to that ! "

———

" My wife is always after me for more money. Every morning it is ' Give me $500 ' and every evening it is ' Give me five hundred more.' "

"What does she do with all the money?"

" I don't know. I haven't given her any yet."

———

" If I was rich as Creosote, I couldn't satisfy that woman."

———

Fields sits down by a counter in the department store and begins weeping over his family troubles. He wipes his eyes on a pair of corsets and absently puts them in his pocket. He is weeping into a pair of silk stockings

when the proprietor sees him. When Fields puts the
stockings in his pocket, the proprietor seizes him and
cries:

"I'll have you put in the calaboose for this."

"Don't call me that!"

"Call you what? Calaboose? You don't know what
a calaboose is."

"Yes I do. It's the last car on a freight train."

———

The shopkeeper pulls open Field's coat and reveals
the stolen stockings in his pocket.

"Good heavens!" Lew exclaims guiltily, "Now I'll
be given ten years for hosiery."

———

"You can act as house detective for me," says the
shopkeeper. "My cashier is spending more money
than he earns. I smell a rat. You must catch him."

"What do you think I am, a piece of cheese?"

———

"Does your wife call you 'Hennery'?"

"If I was to tell you all what my wife calls me, the
company would take the telephone out."

———

"Keep a watch on the soda fountain. That's where
the leak is most likely to be."

———

"If I had a million dollars I would buy me sealskin
underwear with the fuzzy side in."

Customer—" I would like to look at some fancy silk stockings."

Fields—" If you only want to look at 'em, at the foot of the grand stairway is the best place."

SCANLON AND PRESS

" I told your father we expected to be married next month and he was wild."

" What did he say?"

" He wanted to know why we couldn't make it next week."

" They say it's unlucky to postpone a wedding day."

" Not if you keep on doing it."

" I'm said to have one of the best complexions in town."

" Honest?"

" That's none of your business."

" Why don't you marry my brother?"

" First, because he has no brains and he can't ride, dance or play tennis. What could I do with him?"

" But he swims beautifully."

" O, yes. But one can't keep one's husband in an aquarium, you know."

"What's your line of business?"

"I'm an actress."

"I'm disappointed."

"Why?"

"Thought you were a shoplifter."

"Have you seen papa's new dog, Carlo?"

"Yes; I have had the pleasure of meeting the dog the other evening."

"Isn't he splendid? He is so affectionate."

"I noticed he was demonstrative."

"He is very playful, too. I never saw a more playful animal in all my life."

"I am so glad to hear you say that."

"Why?"

"Because I was a little afraid that when he bit that piece out of me the other evening he was in earnest. But if he was only in play of course it's all right. I can take a joke as well as anybody."

"Why do married men talk in their sleep?"

"So as not to forget how, I suppose."

STAN STANLEY AND HIS RELATIVES

"My act won't take long and I don't want any interference from you down in the audience."

"You may be clever, but you fail to interest me. What is your act, anyway?"

"I'm a magician."

"Well, if you're any good at all you can disappear."

"You're not bad. You might do on the stage. What's your vocation, anyway?"

"Vocation—what do you mean?"

" I mean, what do you work at?"

" Work?"

" Yes."

" Who? Me? No!"

" I thought I'd like to have you up here on the stage with me."

" What do you pay?"

" Whatever you're worth."

" You don't want me, mister. I'm a detective."

" A detective?"

" Yes. Do you see these heels?"

" Yes."

" Well, I ran them down."

" Give us a waltz, orchestra leader—a Wilson waltz."

" I don't get you."

" One with lots of good notes in it."

GRACE DE WINTERS AND DUMMY

" Well, what do you want?"

" Lady, I wanta help yer out in singing."

" Help me out in singing? How could you help me out in singing?"

" I was just gonna' sing a Scotch song."

" A Scotch song?"

" Yep."

" Didn't you now that to be able to sing a Scotch song good, you must be Scotch or have a little Scotch in you?"

" Dat's all right, lady, I've got enough Scotch in me, for I just put it in at the corner saloon."

BERT SAVOY AND JAY BRENNAN

" Are you Evelyn Nesbit? "

" No, I'm Evenlyn Wasbit."

" Marjory and I were on the top deck of the ship when it stopped in the middle of the ocean. The

captain then came along and Marjory asked, 'What's a matter?'

" 'The rudder's broke.'

" 'O, that's all right; it's underneath and nobody will notice it.'

" We went to a medium and she said she could see through anything. When I asked Marjory why she ran out she replied: 'I had on a one-piece dress.'"

ADAMS AND GUHL

" Well, how can you find the greatest common divisor? "

" Advertise for it, you ignoramus."

" What kind of United States are you spoking? "

" Why, what is the trouble? "

" You shouldn't say ignoramus. That ain't right."

" No? "

" Of course no."

" Then how you said it? "

" Innohamus."

" O, say, I was just thoughting how nice it is to have it an eduslated man like you around."

" There you go it again. For why you say eduslated? "

" That ain't right, eh? "

" Certainly not, you should said it edubated."

LYDELL AND HIGGINS

" My father is quite a runner."

" I know it; we went through the war together. In one way I am under great obligations to your father."

" How's that? "

" Well, when he was a doctor he saved my life."

" O, is that so? "

" Yes, I sent for him and he didn't come."

" Well, be that as it may, I'm going to sing you  a little song. Father heard it as he was passing a saloon."

" Go on! Your father never passed a saloon in his life! "

JACK AND PHIL KAUFMAN

"Do you remember when you said you'd take me where the bees made honey?"

"Yes."

"Well, you took me. Do you remember that large bee that came buzzin' around me, and lit on my lower lip?"

"Did it hurt when he lit?"

"No, it didn't hurt when he lit, but, my land, when he sat down!"

"What is garlic?"

"It's the breath of a nation."

WEBER AND ELLIOT

"Well, if it isn't my old friend Cohen. How are you, Cohen?"

"Not so good; hope you are the same. Thank you."

"You've still got that foolish way of talking, haven't you? But say, where have you been all these years?"

"I've been on mine way to New York."

"It didn't take you ten years to get to New York, did it?"

"I went there on the B. & O."

"You've got to have your joke all right. But tell me, how did you find New York?"

"I didn't have to look for it. It was there when I arrived."

"You don't understand. What I mean is, how did you like New York?"

"O, how I like New York?"

"Yes, that's it; how did you like it?"

"Not much. It was too tough."

"What was too tough?"

"The steak I got there."

"I'm not talking about the eats. I'm asking you about the city."

"Just the same."

"What do you mean just the same?"

"The city was just the same like the steak."

"I see, New York is a tough city?"

"Yes, tough."

"You shouldn't call a city tough; you should say common."

"Yes, just the same."

"So you enjoyed yourself, did you?"

"Little bit, by me and not very much. I went down by the cellar."

"What did you go down a cellar for?"

"To get on the train."

"You don't mean you went down a cellar; you mean you went down into the subway."

"Yes, just the same."

JIM HALLEY AND JESSE NOBLE

"Talking about large vegetables, I know a man in California that raised a pumpkin so large that his two children use a half each for a cradle."

"That's nothing; we have in this town as many as three policemen sleeping on one beat."

"How plainly you can see the man in the moon!"

"There's a woman in the moon."

"No, there's a man in the moon."

"I tell you there is a woman in the moon."

"How do you know there is a woman in the moon?"

"Do you suppose that man would stay there long if there wasn't a woman up there?"

"Where did a hen's egg come from?"

"From the hen, of course."

"Where did the hen come from?"

"From the egg."

"Who came here first?"

————

"I went in a saloon and ordered two glasses of beer, and it didn't cost me a cent."

"How did you manage it?"

"I drank one and I let the other one settle."

"I can spell bum with two letters."

"Let me hear you."

"B-m, bum."

"That doesn't spell bum."

"O, yes, I forgot and left you out."

"That girl of yours is a sweet kisser."

"How do you know?"

"O, I had it right from her own lips."

BERT WILLIAMS

Recruiting Sergeant—"What's your profession?"

Bert Williams—"I been workin' lately as a draughtsman."

Sergeant—"What d'ye mean by draughtsman?"

Williams—"Whenever Colonel Clayton feels a draught he sends me to find out where it's coming from and shut the window."

Sergeant—"What is your name?"

Williams—"They call me Pat for short."

Sergeant—"Pat? Do you mean to imply that you are Irish?"

Williams—"I don't imply nothing; I'm a Senegambian colored person."

Sergeant—"Then how can they call you Pat for short? What is your full name?"

Williams—"Patagonia Senegambia Washington Lee."

Sergeant—"How much wages have you been getting a month?"

Williams—"Three dollars a week."

Sergeant—"How much is that a month?"

Williams—"'Bout four hundred dollars, I guess."

Sergeant—"You guess? Why don't you know?"

Williams—"'Cause I never saved up my money for a month to find out. I spend my money like a gentleman as fast as I make it."

Sergeant—"You'll get thirteen dollars a month in the army."

Williams—"I'd rather have three dollars a week. I can comprehend it better that way."

Sergeant—"Can you read?"

Williams—"Not without my glasses."

Sergeant—"Astigmatism?"

Williams—"No, Free Methodism, but I've studied a lot about Mormonism."

Sergeant—"That's ambiguous."

Williams—"No, sir. The Mormons don't practice ambiguity any more. One wife is enough for me, and entirely too many."

Sergeant—"We're talking about your eyesight. How far can you see?"

Williams—"If I could see where my next meal was coming from I wouldn't be joining the army."

Sergeant—"If you are near-sighted, how could you keep the Mexicans from sneaking up and surprising you?"

Williams—"I can smell 'em a mile off. The only way the Mexicans could surprise us is by taking a bath. That would not only surprise us, it would astonish us."

Sergeant—"Then there couldn't be any close fighting with the Greasers, eh?"

Williams—"Oh, yes; it would be close. Close in the same sense as when you come home after your neighbors have been cooking fish, cabbage and garlic, and you open a hall window, saying: 'Whew, it's close.'"

Sergeant—"Do you want to join the foot soldiers and walk, the cavalry and ride horseback, or the field artillery and ride on the gun carriage?"

Williams—"I'll join the coast artillery and go coasting."

Sergeant—"How are you on the constitution?"

Williams—"I've got a cast-iron constitution. My wife has cast flat irons at me and never made a dent."

Sergeant—" I mean the United States constitution. Are you familiar with it?"

Williams—" I can't claim to be exactly familiar with it, but I'm friendly with it."

Sergeant—" Are your teeth in good order?"

Williams—" What difference does it make about my teeth; I don't intend to bite the Mexicans; I'll use the bayonet. Let me be the man that carves them; I don't care who eats 'em."

Sergeant—" You shall be the color sergeant."

Williams—" Yes, sir; I'll be a colored sergeant."

Sergeant—" And you shall bear the flag in battle with your two strong arms; the beauteous banner that has never dipped before the foe. And when one arm is shot away, you shall seize the flag in the other and press gloriously on. And when both arms are gone—"

Williams—" Yes?"

Sergeant—" You still scorn to drop the flag of your country. It's starry folds still kissing the breeze, you bear it along the front of battle until both your legs are shot off, and still—"

Williams—" Still I can't kick."

Sergeant—" And when your head is carried off by a cannon ball—"

Williams—" Say, how long is this battle goin' to last?"

Sergeant—" The flag is everything! The flag is all; why think of anything else? Old Glory is the stake for which—"

Williams—" Yes, but yuh cain't eat that kind of steak."

Sergeant—" And when you've died for the flag you will be happy to—"

Williams—"Yes, I'll be glad to be dead after a battle like that."

Sergeant—"And you will be buried with military honors and great pomp and show."

Williams—"What good is a show when the audience is dead?"

Sergeant—"And the chaplain will say the last—"

Williams—"Aw, he can't make me laugh any more."

Sergeant—"Who can't."

Williams—"Charlie Chaplin."

Sergeant—"And so you will die for honor and glory instead of living the useless life of a loafer. Hades is full of crooked cards, dice, women and gin."

Williams—"What! Is Hades full of all of those tempting things?"

Sergeant—"Absolutely."

Williams—"Oh, Death, where is thy sting?"

CHARLES REILY

Don't blame me for the temper I display tonight, for it surely isn't on my account, because I'm real sour this evening. Yes, real sour. If there is one thing I dislike it is a man who tries to be witty. I just stopped in a butcher shop a while ago and asked him for a piece of beef for roasting. The meat, mostly all bone, he threw on the scales, so I said to him: "Look here, sir, you are giving me a big piece of bone."

"Oh, no, I ain't," answered the butcher, "you're going to pay for it."

And not only all that, but I sent for a gas man last night because the pipes needed looking after. I told the gas company's inspector that there was a leak somewhere and a big lot of gas was going to waste. He thought for a minute, and then replied in a somewhat cunning voice: "Perhaps there is a leak, but there ain't any gas going to waste; you will find it all on the bill."

JAMES J. CORBETT

Shortly after one of my ring battles I met Steve Brodie, the man who jumped off the Brooklyn bridge. I told my father about him, and suggested that he come with me and be introduced to him. I told him that it would be a nice thing to say that he had met and talked with the only man who ever jumped off the Brooklyn bridge, so finally the old man grudgingly consented.

When the introduction was effected the old man looked Brodie over from crown to toe. "And you're the felly that jumped over the Brooklyn bridge," he said.

"No, no, Mr. Corbett," Brodie hastened to correct him, "I didn't jump over. I jumped off!"

"Jumped off!" exclaimed father. "Anny dang fool could do that!"

Once, after coming out of a theater shortly after the famous battle when Fitzsimmons put me out, I heard two little boys discussing me, my fight, and my solar plexus.

"It's on the left side," said one little fellow.

"Go on!" the other contradicted. "It's on the right."

Thus they argued for several minutes, and when then saw me (although they did not recognize me) they made me a judge. The more mild of the two came up and asked me what side the solar plexus was on. After telling them who I was I explained that the solar plexus was neither on the left or right side, but in the middle.

"What does he know about it!" yelled the youngster who had championed the right side. "He was asleep when it all happened."

JAS. T. DUFFY AND MERCEDES LORENZ

"How old are you?"

"I am going on 16."

"Go on, go on!"

"Let us go to the opera tonight."

"Fine! What is the bill going to be?"

"About $11 I think."

"Last night I had a dream."

"What did you dream?"

"I dreamed that you were passionately in love with me. What is that a sign of?"

"That's a sign that you were dreaming."

RAY AND GORDON DOOLEY AND ELMER GRAHAM

" What's that sticking out of your collar?"

" I don't see anything."

" Ah, yes, it's your head."

" How long does it take you to dress?"

" Twenty minutes."

" Twenty minutes? I do it in ten."

" Yes, but I wash."

" Good evening, Alice."

" What do you mean, 'Alice'?"

" Why, I'm just showing you how I'd propose."

" Very well."

" Good evening, Alice; I have come on bended knee to give you my heart."

" Get away; I have liver in the icebox."

FRANKLIN ARDELL

(Imitating a Real Estate Faker)

" Here we have some of the finest lots in the world, forty minutes' ride from the city and beautiful at low tide. Submarines run every hour. The chance of a lifetime to build your own home. Now here is a beautiful lot, 25x100 feet. How much am I offered? Twenty-five cents! How much is that for a beautiful lot? Do I hear fifty? Fifty, a dollar. Two dollars.

Two and a half. Two and a half, two and a half, two and a half—sold to Mr. Ginsburg for two and a half. Two dollars' profit! Boy, wrap up a lot for Mr. Ginsburg. Better give it to him in a pail.

"Now, gentlemen, who would like to live next door to Mr. Ginsburg? I have a beautiful lot. How much am I offered? Do I hear right? Three fifty! Put that in writing!

"Ah, here's a letter: 'Dear Mr. Simpson: When you sold me those two lots you said they were forty minutes from the city, but you forgot to mention what city. Please wire immediately. Yours truly, A. Smith.'"

NANCY FAIR

When Mike first came to the city he wrote his girl a letter. She's a nice girl—works for a good family in the village as a servant. Well, Mike wrote the letter, and then went to mail it in the city postoffice.

When Mike entered the postoffice he paused in perplexity before a board containing three slots bearing the words, "City," "Domestic," "Foreign."

"Faith," muttered Mike, "this is a fine fix to be in. Molly's a domestic, she lives in the city, and she's a foreigner. What gets me is, how am I to get the letter into the three holes at once?"

KRAMAR AND MERTON

" You're not good looking; your mouth is too big."

" Well, yours is no buttonhole."

" I'll bet I can make a funnier face than you can."

" I'll bet you ten dollars you can't."

" Won't take you; the bet's off. I changed my mind."

" Why? "

" Well, look at the start you've got! "

" That's enough of that. You pull any more of that stuff and I'll climb your frame, one, two, three. Get me? One, two, three! "

" Four, five, six, you'll climb right off again! "

" What is an icicle? "

" An icicle is a stiff piece of water."

" What is the principal thing made of ivory? "

" I'm looking at it."

MARIE CAHILL

When I was down in Texas I saw a baptism. There was one Negro, a great poker player, that came within the minister's grasp. As he was led out into the water the ace of diamonds floated out of his vest, then the king, queen, jack, and ten. The preacher's eyes bulged wide. " Man," he exclaimed, " if that hand doesn't save you there's no use bein' baptized! "

I'm sorry I got here so late. But I had trouble with my dress. Not this one—the other one. My husband got tired of hooking it up and I had to finish it myself. Even a hook worm will turn, you know.

We gave a luncheon the other day. It was very swell. We had Caruso and Farrar and Gorgonzola. We had them to sing, not for lunch. Then we had a harp player. She sat there looking like the "Gates Ajar." I didn't care much for her playing, although she is said to be good. In fact they say she is one of the best known harpies on the stage.

ROBERTS AND STUART

"Did you hear about Isaacstein?"

"No, what about him?"

"He was in a railroad accident and got his right foot cut off."

"Poor Isaacstein."

"Yes, that fellow has been having the worst luck."

"Why so?"

"Just before the accident he bought twenty-five cents worth of corn plaster."

"Still he can use the corn plaster for the other foot, can't he?"

"Yes, but that wouldn't be right."

"Why wouldn't it be right?"

"Because it'd be left. The right one got cut off."

WATSON SISTERS

"You're jealous of my figure."

"That's no figure; it's a number."

"I've got a beau who says I'm worth my weight in gold."

"I didn't think there was that much money in the world."

"How do you like this yellow dress of mine?"

"Extremely becoming."

"Yes, I wear it 364 days out of the year."

"Why not the three hundred and sixty-fifth?"

"That's St. Patrick's day and I want to live."

"What do you think of a man who will constantly deceive his wife and get away with it all the time?"

"What do I think of him? I think he's a wonder!"

"We'll take our flowers now. There's no fun at the graveyard."

ELSA RYAN

"What are husbands?"

"Husbands are little things that run around flats."

HARRY ANTRIM AND BETSY VALE

" I'm knockkneed."

" Yes, I noticed."

" My brother's bowlegged."

" How unfortunate."

" Yes, when we stand together we spell ' ox.' "

" Is that a vaccination mark? "

" Sir, I'll have you understand I wasn't vaccinated there."

" Where were you vaccinated? "

" In Elgin."

PAUL McCARTY AND ELSIE FAYE

" No, I'm not drinking anything. I'm on the wagon."

" Still? "

" No, restless."

" Where shall we live? "

" In the old house. I'll have my maid and you'll have your valet."

" O, you mean Hill? "

" Yes."

" Isn't that funny that a man named Hill should be a valet? "

" It is. Is he still with you? "

" No, I had to let him go; he wasn't on the level."

NORWOOD AND HALL

"I wish you would mind your own business when I'm talking to any one."

"I can't; I've got all I can do to attend to yours."

"Say, where have you been for a week?"

"I've been to the lamp store."

"What for?"

"Why, for a wick."

"Say, why don't you settle down and take a wife?"

"I would, but I don't know whose wife to take."

"My wife stole a cradle today."

"What for?"

"O, just for a kid."

"Say, I'm in a new business now."

"What line?"

"Clothes line, at night."

"We were going so fast we smashed into another team and it took a wheel off the dog's tail."

"Nonsense; who ever heard of a wheel on a dog's tail? Wagons have wheels."

"Well, this dog's tail was a-waggin'."

"Did you know the old man was dead?"

"Is that so? What complaint?"

"No complaint; everybody satisfied."

EDDIE ROSS

Dere's something dats been occupyin' my mind foh a long time. Maybe you've figgahed it out. Have you evah noticed dat dere's so many moah people in towns of a lahge population than dere is in towns of a small population? I asked mah wife and eben she couldn't tell me, and she's an uncommonly smaht woman. Mah wife shoah was a smaht woman, in fack she was about all right. She was a little slim, even a little slimmer, if ah may say so, than I am. She wouldn't weigh moah than fohty pounds soakin' wet. She was skinnier than a vegetarian's hat. When she was dressed in a white dress she didn't dare drink no cullud drinks. Once she had on a white dress and drank some red lemonade and she looked just like a thermometer.

We had a Dutch hound. He was about a dog and a half long and about half a dog high. Dat dog neber had no bringin' up. Ah' was down dere when dey was bringin' him up. Dey always kept him down when dey was bringin' him up. Dey raised him under the bureau.

Ah was born at a very early age, in fack it was in mah early childhood, in a private family. Mah parents were dere at the time, ah believe, though ah'm not suah. Ah was originally triplets. Ah remember father came staggering home and asked my mother which one ob us three she wanted to keep as he was goin' to drown the other two. There was an awful lot of children in our family; there was foahteen of dem dat we was persoonally acquainted with and ah don't know how many moah there was. Once three of dem got lost and we nevah missed dem till dey showed up three months later.

The other two triplets was named Frank and Henry. Frank and Henry was so much alike dat mah mother couldn't tell 'em apaht. In fack, if it hadn't been foah my brother, Skunkton, mah mother would nevah have been able to tell them apaht. One day my brother Skunkton was out in the yahd and Frank bit him and he came in and my mother said, "Skunky, who bit you?" and Skunkton said Frank bit him, so mother said, "Well then Frank must be the one with teeth."

MEDLIN, WATTS AND TOWNES

"Where's the party you married?"

"I didn't marry a party—I married one."

"Did you marry well?"

"Yes, she has a fine job."

"Are you going to sing?"

"Yes, a little ballad entitled, 'Don't Worry About the Wood, Mamma, Father Will Bring Home a Load.'"

" You pull another con like that and I'll close your eye for you."

" You do and there'll be singing at your house, but you won't hear it."

" How do you like married life? "

"Great! You know, I'm king in my house."

" Yes. I was there the night she crowned you."

" Well, I must be getting on. I'm going to treat my wife."

" How? "

" O, I'm going to take her up to her mother's."

JOSEPH E. BERNARD AND COMPANY IN "WHO IS SHE?"

" If you ever cross this threshold again it will be over my dead body."

" Say that over again; it sounds funny."

" How long have we been married? "

" Nine weeks."

" It seems like a thousand years to me."

" Believe me, it does! "

" Now listen here, a married man has no right— "

" I know it—not a one."

" O, you're horrid."

" But I want to explain. This Pearl isn't a woman, but a man. I've told you that a dozen times already."

"I don't believe you!"

"All right, then you can go to—"

"Don't you tell me where you told the iceman to go this morning."

"Well, what would you do if I did?"

"I'll tell you! I'll show you! I'm going to leave this house—for good!"

"Good! O, why is there a law preventing husbands from killing their wives!"

WOOD, BELL AND WOOD

"What nationality are you?"

"That is what has been troubling me for a long while. My father was an Italian and my mother was a Turk; I was born on an English ship in Chinese waters under the French flag. Now, you'll have to tell me what I am."

"It's hard to tell what you are. What is your nationality? Where were you born?"

"Well, I am crossed between the sun and the moon. I get mooney once in a while."

"You don't seem to understand me, so let me explain. Wherever a person is born, that is his place of nativity. Now, we'll say a man is born in Boston; what is he?"

"He's a nativity."

"No, no; he is a Bostonian. Now, a man born in Washington, what is he?"

"He's a man that does washing."

"Certainly not; he is a Washingtonian. Now if a man is born in Michigan, he is a Michigander."

GAYLORD AND LANGTON

"I saw you passing my office today."

"Your office! That ash barrel."

"I saw you cleaning out your office with a poker."

"No; I keep a drug store. I am a doctor and druggist."

"We belong to the same fraternity."

"Do you know anything about medicine?"

"I ought to know something about medicine. I used to take care of a doctor's horse."

"Me, too; I know all about medicine. I washed the doctor's wagon."

"Then you know something about materia medica. You are well versed in medicine. Now, let me ask you a question. Suppose a Dutch baker was going along the street and should slip and fall and sprain his back, what would you call that?"

"A Dutch twist."

" If a dude should fall and sprain his wrist, what would you call that? "

" A monkey wrench."

" Now, in case of accident, a man should poison himself, what would you do? "

" Let him die."

" No; scrape the plaster from the wall, for lime is an antidote. If you should see a man hanging, what would you do? "

" Cut him down."

" Medically speaking."

" Cut him up."

" If a man would walk into your office with a raging toothache, what would you do? "

" Pull his tooth."

" If he had a sprained ankle? "

" Pull his leg."

DALE AND ARCHER

" Well, here he is now, my old friend, Mr. Hickory."

" What do you mean by calling me by such a name as Hickory? You know well enough that Hickory is not my name. How did you ever come to name me such a name? "

" The only reason for me calling you Hickory is because you look so much like a nut. But, say, where have you been all last month that I didn't see you? "

" I've been down to my bungalow."

" You don't mean to say you call that old joint of a shack of yours a bungalow? "

" If it isn't a bungalow, what is it? The job was a bungle and I still owe for it, so bungalow is the only name I can give it."

GERTRUDE VANDERBILT AND
GEORGE MOORE

"Well, general, how do you feel today?"

"I feel full."

"How full?"

"Awful."

———

"Can you tell me what's good for hives?"

"Certainly — bees."

"Ha, ha! Where did you get that one?"

"O, I bought that one."

"You got stung. By the way, who was that little girl I saw you walking down the street with the other day?"

"O, she was a little hungry girl I met somewhere. I gave her $500 and told her to get herself a sandwich at the Kragstone hotel."

"Why didn't you make it a thousand so the poor girl could have some butter on her bread?"

———

"So you're a soldier, eh? Salute me and come here and take these orders."

"Ha, I'm back on the old job again. What'll you have? Would you like some golden soup?"

"Golden soup? What's that?"

"Fourteen carrots. And how will you have your eggs?"

"What do you mean?"

"Turned or looking at you."

"Now I want you to return to your regiment the worst way."

"It shall be as you say; I'll go over the Clark street bridge."

ANDY RICE

This is the first adversity of my marriage, and I've learned a lot of things. They will tell you that two can live cheaper than one. I do not believe it. Before I was married I made $18 a week, lived like a king, and saved $12. Since I got married I only save ten.

I never intended to marry my wife. I was making love to her sister Rosalie. Rosalie's father owned a liquor store, but he used to be in the saloon business. A very successful man. He has been in bankruptcy twice—yes, a very successful man. Anyhow, I went to talk to him about Rosalie, and he gave me a cigar, took a good one out of the box for himself, and when he had finished talking to me I was engaged to marry Jennie—that's Rosalie's older sister.

But what made me strong for Jennie's father was that just after I got to the house before the wedding he gave me a check for $1,000. After the ceremony he came to me and said:

"Son, there should be no secrets between us now, should there?"

"No, father," I said.

"My secrets are your secrets, and your secrets are my secrets, ain't they?"

"Yes," I said.

"Well, Andy," he answered, "that check I gave you ain't no good."

AVELING AND LLOYD

"Do you remember Bill, the fellow that used to be a butcher back home?"

"Sure I do."

"Well, I saw him a few minutes ago. He's gone into the tailor business."

"Who'd suspect it?"

"Yes, Bill's a tailor; he made me this suit of clothes."

"He's still a butcher, then."

"I've got a friend that wants to introduce me to a wicked blonde."

"How old is she?"

"She used to be 20."

" Well, as for me, I'm a hard luck guy when it comes to women. Every one I meet is either hungry or half dead."

" Too bad."

" Yes, I have to either buy 'em dinner or give 'em car fare, and they all live in Australia! What's that you have there?"

" That's a bill. He's the last member of the family. He's just ten. And now he's going away. I always call him Bill."

" Is that his Christian name?"

" I don't think so; you always find bills in Jewish families. Poor little bill, he hasn't any father or mother. He's all alone. I'll never forget how his father died."

" How was that?"

" His father died trying to make a nine—with the dice."

———

" Speaking of reincarnation, I remember when I was a minnow and you were an oyster."

" Yes, that was in the fish age."

" Again, I remember when you were a frankfurter and I was a hot dog."

" That was in the sausage."

" And when you were cold chicken and I was an egg."

" That was in the cold storage."

" And I remember, too, when you were a carrot and I was an onion."

" So do I; that was in the garbage."

BEN WELCH

I vas to meet her here at haluf past six. It is now five o'clock. While I'm vaiting for her, I'll go home.

How do you like my new Prince Isaac coat? Look at the goods; that's a fine piece of merchandise. I got it in a restaurant. The feller's still eating.

Everybody is riding in a cheap motor car these days. I've got it a motor car myself. It's an E. M. F. Every morning fix it.

I went to a pinochle party last night and my vife von der prize. Two soup plates. Mit der name Pullman on 'em.

I have wrote a motion picture skeenario. It vas passed by der lumber board. A child vas abandoned in der Cowskills Mountains. His father had been driven to drunk. He left home in a light snowstorm. It used to be a heavy snowstorm, but der price of paper has gone up on account of the war.

The reason he vas driven to drunk vas because his vife was a Wampire Woman.

Der child in der Cowskills grows up and goes vest to make his fortune. He gets a job as bookkeeper in a shooting gallery.

Mit honesty and industry he rises. At last he marries der foreman's daughter.

In dis play there vas seven characters—maybe nine —who knows?

I vill now tell a dillydaff. You know vat was a dillydaff? I am a doctor and you say: "Oh, doctor, I'm sick."

Orchestra leader: "Oh, doctor, I'm sick."

I ain't got it time for you now, I'm on my way to attend der Birth of a Nation.

I've bought it a house in the suburbs already. If you live in the city rent eats you up. If you live in the country mosquitoes eat you up. My house is near the village of Malaria Junction.

Two hours' walk, after you take the street car.

As far as the eye could reach, castoria signs.

A large bingelow, mit eleven rooms and two vindows. A bedroom so large I can change my shirt in it mitout going outdoors.

Two kinds of vater; dirty and clean. Steam in der steam pipes—in July.

Put a quarter in der meter and have gas for a veek.

I've had gas for two months! I got a quarter mit a string on it.

My vife complains they ain't no vindow shades. She says the neighbors will see her if she takes a bath.

I told her to go ahead and take the bath, and if the neighbors see her they will buy the vindow shades.

A friend wanted me to lend him $10 without no security. I said, "What guarantee I got you ever pay me back? What if you'd drop dead on me?"

He said: "I wouldn't do such a dirty trick."

The feller's a slick feller. He used to keep company mit my vife the same time I did. Any man what's smarter than me I don't want to do no business with him.

My oldest boy is seventeen years old. He smokes oakum. He asks has anybody got change for a million dollars. Last night he bought St. Louis.

He has a little silver pencil he sticks in his wrist.

Last time he stuck it in his arm he was elected governor. He stuck it in my arm, and I paid the rent.

MR. AND MRS. JIMMIE BARRIE

"Sy Terwilliger, the editor of the Henville Hornet, is certainly a great editor."

"How's that?"

"Well, he came right out and contradicted the New York Evening Journal the other day."

"What happened?"

"Well, up until a day ago he hadn't received any reply."

"I went down to New York for two weeks."

"How much did you get trimmed for?"

"It wasn't like that at all; in fact, I made my expenses."

"Why, how?"

"Well, everybody knew I was a rube just to look at me. So I went around and bought eggs for 15 cents a dozen and sold them as strictly fresh country eggs for 50 cents a dozen."

LONEY HASKELL

The other day I saw Mrs. Murphy again. I am reminded of a story about her. Once she went to the dentist to have a tooth extracted.

"Will you have gas?" the dentist inquired.

"You bet your life I'll have gas," she exclaimed. "Catch the widow Murphy stayin' in a room wid' a strange man without gas!"

Going down in the car for my dinner, I turned to the conductor and said: "Do you stop at the Blackstone?" He turned and looked at me, then said: "Not on my wages, mister."

When I finally reached the restaurant I heard a man ask for soup—oxtail soup. "Gee," said the waitress, "that's going a long way back for soup!"

After she had finished with him she went up to a little Jew and said: "What's your order?" The Jew threw back the lapel of his coat and cried, "Independent Free Sons of Israel!"

At last she came to another man and asked him if he wished for coffee. "Great guns!" exclaimed the man, "do you have to wish for it?"

There is a story I know about Rosenbaum. Rosenbaum had sold Cassidy a consignment of goods, allowing him sixty days in which to pay. When the time was up Cassidy had not paid and Rosenbaum sent him the following letter:

"Mr. Cassidy, dear sir: Who bought some goods from my store sixty days ago? You!

"Who promised to pay for them at the end of that time and didn't pay? You!

"Who is a liar, a thief, and a scoundrel? Yours truly,

      "Abe Rosenbaum."

BERT FITZGIBBON

"Well, Harry, I've got a riddle for you. There was a little dog with a crooked tail running down the street

with no one behind him. Now, what was the little dog running down the street for?"

"I'm sure I don't know, Bert."

"Well, Harry, he was in a hurry. And, by the way, Harry, I got a great piece of news today, a welcome message from my old home town."

"What was the message, Bert?"

"It said: 'Come home; your tailor is dead!' Now I've got another story to tell you. It's about a policeman and another Irishman. The policeman arrested the Irishman on a corner, and as they were waiting for the wagon the Irishman's hat blew off. 'Let me go and get it. I'll come back,' begged the Irishman. The policeman laughed. 'G'wan,' he said. 'Me let you go and git yer hat? Not me! Ye'd never come back.' The Irishman insisted that he wouldn't run away. The officer shook his head. 'Sure,' he said, 'I wouldn't take the chance. You stand here and I'll go get it.'

"I have another story, Harry. It's about a little girl. Her mother gave her a pitcher and a nickel and sent her after some milk. Pretty soon the little girl came back and said she had broken the pitcher. 'I should beat you,' said her mother. 'But I won't this time.' So she gave her another pitcher and started her off. Pretty soon the little girl came back and said: 'Mother, I've broken the pitcher again.' Her mother looked at her and said: 'I should spank you good, but this time I'll forgive you.' So she gave her another pitcher.

"About fifteen minutes later the child came back with the same story and again her mother reprimanded her, gave her another one and sent her out again. Soon after the child returned and said: 'Mother, I did not break the pitcher, but I lost the nickel.' Her mother was angry and said: 'I should beat you, but I will not do it this time.' Thereupon she gave her another nickel and sent her out again. Two times after that the girl came back with neither pitcher nor nickel. 'I ought to spank you for that,' said her mother, who was a patient woman.

"Thereupon she gave the child another pitcher and another nickel and said: 'My dear, mother is very cross now, and if you come back again without either pitcher or nickel I'll kill you!'

"The little girl went out, but pretty soon she returned. 'I am sorry, mother,' she said, 'but I have lost the nickel and the pitcher, too."

"So her mother killed her."

BEN HARNEY

A conductor in New York city was discharged for knocking down. Three days after that he committed murder; he was arrested, tried, and condemned to die

by electricity. When the day came to electrocute him the apparatus wouldn't work and they couldn't kill him. He was a nonconductor. I don't feel very well this evening; I fell out of bed last night. A friend of mine said I must have slept too near where I got in, but I didn't; I slept too near where I fell out.

Jacob Rosinstine killed a person and got arrested for murder, and it happened he had a friend on the jury, Mr. Isaac Polinski. He managed to have an interview with him and told him on the quiet if he could bring in the verdict of murder in the second degree he would give him $500. The jury was out for three days and at last brought in a verdict of murder in the second degree. Jacob met Polinski after the trial and wanted to know why the jury was out so long. Polinski told him: "I was bound to win that $500. There was eleven wanted acquittal; I wanted second degree."

How to tell a single man from a married one: The single man has no buttons on his shirt; the married man has no shirt. I wore a pillowslip for six months.

When I married my wife she was 24 years old; her mother said she would have been 28, but she was in jail four years.

Tompkins went to a masquerade ball the other evening; the doortender after 12 o'clock asked him to take off his mask. Tompkins said: "I haven't any on."

WILLARD AND BOND

"Did you know a person could get drunk on water?"

"Impossible; you can't get drunk on water."

"I don't see why a person can't get drunk on water as well as on land."

"Women are the ruination of men."

"You shouldn't talk of women that way. Remember, when a man is sick woman is always found at his bedside."

"Yes—going through his pockets for loose change."

"Say, I think you're the finest looking man I ever saw."

"I'm sorry I can't return the compliment."

"You could if you told as big a lie as I did."

"Do you know Bill Smith?"

"Yes; what about him?"

"He had his hand cut off almost to the wrist."

"That was too bad."

"Best thing ever happened."

"How so?"

"He was only getting two dollars a day; now he is getting five."

"How is that?"

"Shorthand writer."

———

"How do you like married life?"

"O, I live like a bird."

"How is that?"

"I have to fly for my life."

———

CRANSTON AND LEE

"I understand you are separated from your wife."

"Yes."

"Tell me all about it. What did you do?"

"Nothing. She died."

"What's the difference between a pretty girl's mouth and a couple of impertinent country fellows?"

"I give it up."

"One is a pair of ruby lips, and the others a pair of lippy rubes."

"They say that famous marine artist was once a plain farmer's boy. I wonder where he developed his talent?"

"Drawing water on the farm."

"What kind of leather makes the best shoes?"

" Don't know, but banana skins make good slippers."

" It's funny, isn't it, that everybody in our family is some kind of an animal?"

" Some kind of an animal, indeed? What do you mean?"

" Why, mother is a dear, you know."

" Yes, certainly."

" And my baby sister is mother's little lamb, and I'm he kid, and dad's the goat."

FENTELL AND STARK

I saw you coming out of a barroom to-day.

I had to come out some time.

Do you know where Susie Brown lives, that keeps a laundry?

I know where she does washing, but I don't know where she hangs out.

I will have some soup.

Give me the same.

And some oysters.

Give me the same.

Fentell ordered everything he wanted and Stark ordered the same; at last Fentell said: Order me a bootblack, please.

Stark—Bring me the same.

Waiter—Won't one do for the two?

Stark—No, it won't; if he can eat one, I can.

Fentell—I always tell my wife everything that happens.

Stark—That's nothing; I tell my wife lots of things that never happen.

What is capital and labor?

Suppose I loan you ten dollars.

Yes.

That's capital; and if I try to get it back, that's labor.

That's a nice suit of clothes; what did you pay for it?

Sixty days and costs.

———

"I saw a wonderful operation today; the surgeon took a lung out of a man."

"That's nothing; I know a wife that left her husband, and she took the heart out of him."

"Do you know that bowlegged man that comes down Main street every day about 12 o'clock?"

"O, yes."

"He stole my watch and chain yesterday."

"I always thought he was crooked."

———

FREAR AND BAGGOTT

"I went hunting down south and I accidentally rushed into a den of snakes, and, strange to say, not one of them bit me."

"How is that?"

"They were all rattled."

" I saw you out driving the other day.   That was a very spirited animal you had."

" The fastest in the world."

" What is his name? "

" Brains."

" Brains? I never heard of him."

" He always comes in ahead."

TYLER AND CROLIUS

" I want you to be my wife."

" What? "

" You heard me, and I mean every word of it, too. I ain't a bad fellow  at heart—just a little spoilt."

" It all seems like a dream."

" Let me be the light of your life."

" I don't want a light that goes out every night."

" I'll be your steady flame."

" That sounds promising."

" You'll have my presence ever near."

" I hope your presents won't come from the 5 and 10 cent store."

" Nothing like that."

" I wonder if I could really get to like you. I would never marry a man who doesn't make his own living."

" Oh, I've got a job in father's business."

" How much do you earn? "

"Fifty dollars a week."

"Why, $50 a week is all right."

"Yes, $50 a week is what I earn—but $7 is what I get."

JIM HALLEY AND JESSE NOBLE

"I lost a good umbrella today."

"Did you leave it some place?"

"No; the owner saw it and recognized it."

"Did you hear about the two colored baseball clubs playing a very exciting game?"

"No, I did not."

"There were as many razors in the air as there were flies; it was impossible for the umpire to decide the game."

"Why; on account of the fight?"

"No, no, not on account of the fight."

"Why couldn't the umpire decide the game?"

"He had to call the game on account of darkness."

"Mike, Mike," cried Hogan, "stop scratchin' yer head, b'y."

"I won't; they began on me first," answered Mike.

"Why, Dennis," said Patrick, "how did they come to naturalize you? Shure an' you haven't been here long enough to get your papers."

"Ah, it was the natural lies I told them that made them naturalize me."

———

"Dennis, I'm told ye was the best man at Mike's marriage."

"The same is a lie," answered Dennis, "but be-javers, I was as good as any man was there."

———

A young Irishman asked a widow to marry him.

"What's the difference between meself and Willard Pond's cow?" asked the widow.

"I don't know," said the Irishman.

"Then," said the widow, "you'd better marry the cow."

———

Casey said to Riley: "You stop outside this saloon till I clean the place out. There's about a dozen loafers in there that needs a trimming. As I throw 'em through the door, you count 'em." Casey entered the saloon and in about a minute a man comes flying through the door into the street.

Riley cried in a loud voice:

"One!"

"Shut up, you fool," answered Casey. "It's me."

———

"Moike," said Terence, "did yez put out the cat?"

"Oi did."

"Oi don't belave it."

"Well, if yez t'ink Oi'm a loiyer, g'wan an' put her out yersilf!"

NEIL McKINLEY

Lately my mother-in-law has gotten the dancing craze and upon me devolves the pleasant duty of teaching her some of the latest steps. She weighs 300 pounds—400 on an ice scale—and yet I find it no more difficult to push her around the ballroom floor than if I were moving a piano.

The other night I showed her a new dance, "The Banana Flop." And flop we did—me underneath. I broke three ribs—and a New Year's resolution. My, but she got angry. She said: "I don't know what to call you." I said, "Call me an ambulance."

Last Thursday we all went to a Sunday school picnic. It was held in a beautiful spot called Mosquito Grove. The tickets were $3 each, including the boat ride, admission to the park, and poison oak. A special boat had been hired for the occasion. My mother-in-law was the heaviest person on board, so they used her for ballast. There was also a band of music. After every selection they passed around the hat. But after a while some of the passengers got so seasick that they were afraid to risk the hat any more.

After a pleasant sail of two hours—although it didn't seem over seven—our scow finally came in sight of Mosquito Grove. And then came the trouble of landing. The captain was cock-eyed. He looked where he was going. But he didn't go where he was looking. So he ran the front of the scow into the side of the wharf. And it just jarred the passengers so hard that it shook out all my mother-in-law's teeth. I let a little boy pick them up. I was afraid if I stooped down for them myself they might bite me.

J. C. NUGENT AND JULE YORK

(Nugent plays part of intoxicated man)

"This must be the doctor's office. I should have seen a doctor in the first place. The trouble is, there wasn't a doctor in the first place, and by the time I got to the last place I didn't need a doctor in the first place."

"How did you get in here? The front door is locked."

"I presume I came in the side door."

"Why should you come in the side door?"

"I suppose I thought it was Sunday."

"Well, what do you want?"

"I want to see the doctor."

"I don't think you need any medicine."

"I don't like medicine. I like patent medicines, but I don't like real medicine."

"What is your trouble?"

"In my knees mostly."

"Is your trouble in the joints?"

"That's where it started."

"In which one?"

"I think it was Hennessy's."

"When did you first notice it?"

"Not until after we got to Murphy's."

"Then you are paralyzed?"

"Not now; but I was earlier in the evening."

"Do you want me to treat you?"

"What have you got?"

"Come into the consultation room."

"Bring it out here; I've got an opener."

"Here, drink this water."

"Be careful and don't spill it. They say it's very nice to skate on when it's hard."

"Your case seems to justify emergency methods."

"Don't call a patrol."

"I wish to test your motor reflexes."

"She thinks I'm a flivver."

ELSIE JANIS, IMITATING FRANK TINNEY

"I'm going to recite serious poetry, I am. Now you must ask me why I am going to recite serious poetry. Go ahead and ask me."

"All right. Why are you going to recite serious poetry, Frank?"

"Because I'm ambitious, I am."

"I don't think it's ambition; I think it's a hang-over."

"O, no, it isn't a hangover. Now you ask me why it isn't a hangover, and I'll answer you. Now this is going to be dirty. Go ahead and ask me."

"Well, why isn't it a hangover, Frank?"

"Because I was out with you last night, and it was your time to treat."

BEN RYAN AND HARRIETTE LEE

"What business are you in?"

"I get $200 a week in the lumber business."

"You have a great head for the lumber business."

"Do you know you have wonderful teeth?"

"Oh, do you think so?"

"Yes, where did you get them?

Now tell me something. Do you love me?"

"Ask me something sensible."

"O, that's not kind. Especially when I've bought you a nice present for your birthday."

"O, did you buy me a present?"

"Certainly, but may be you'd rather have the dollar."

HONEYBOY MINSTRELS

"Why do they play football in the fall?"

"Because nuts don't get ripe until autumn."

"I was up to a dance the other night, Mr. Interlocutor."

"That so, Mr. Bones. What did you do?"

"I got real angry."

"For what reason?"

"My gal was up there with another man."

"And what did you do, Bones?"

"I cut her acquaintance—yes, sir, I cut him good!"

WESTON AND WESTON

"Are you fond of a joke?"

"Why, I hardly know you."

"I mean a joke that you laugh at."

"You're the funniest thing I've seen lately."

"You don't know what an impression you've made on me."

"And you don't know what an impression my big brother will make on you when I tell him you've been trying to flirt with me."

"Your big brother had better be careful. I'm somewhat of a boxer."

"What boxing have you ever done?"

"I used to box cigars for a tobacco company."

WILL H. FOX

There's been a rumor going around that I was dead.
But it was another fellow. I knew it wasn't me the
minute I heard about it. I think the report was spread
by a couple of children. When I get married I ain't
going to have any
children. My
mother didn't have
any, either.

And here's an-
other thing. I hate
fresh street car
conductors. The
other day I got on
a Madison street
trolley car and I
said to the con-
ductor: "Can I go
to State street
without change?"
He said: "No, you need a nickel." So I gave him a
lead 5 cent piece. He said: "I can't accept that." I
said: "Then give it to the company."

Last week I was in a butcher shop when an old maid
came in and said to the butcher, "Is your steak tender?" He said: "Madam, it's as tender as a woman's
heart." She said: "Then give me mutton-chops."

ALF GRANT

"Speaking of life and happiness, I overheard a man asking his neighbor in a street car if he ever reflected on the shortness of life, the uncertainty of all things here below, and the fact that death is inevitable.

"'Have I?' replied the man who was sitting next to the inquirer. 'Well, I should say I have. I'm a life insurance agent.' See what he means?

"But there is a funny thing about life. Take, for instance, women. What good would life be without them? Then, on the other hand, what good is life when you've got one? See what I mean?

"Then another thing about life. Take, for instance, an appetite. Now, we all know every one wishes for one, but still, when they get it they try to get rid of it.

"Then another thing about life. Take vacation in the summer and you stop at a boarding house in New Jersey. New Jersey has educated mosquitoes. They wouldn't bite an ordinary bum or rummy for fear they'd get soused. I'll never forget the summer I went to New Jersey for my vacation. Well, I didn't exactly go to New Jersey on my vacation; I went there on a train when I took my vacation. I also took my grip along, too. The first night I couldn't get to sleep. The mosquitoes bit me up so terribly. But the following night I worked up a scheme, and, believe me, it certainly worked fine. Why, I had all of the mosquitoes perched on the footbar of my bed, and they were coughing like mad. You see, all I had to do was light my pipe and blow a cloud of smoke under the bed covers. That's all. See what I mean?"

KIRK AND FOGARTY

"Who sent me this bunch of flowers?"

"A gentleman in the audience."

"How did you know he was a gentleman?"

"He had a white shirt on."

"Well, it's certainly nice to be revived by these flowers; I've been unconscious all week."

"Is it possible?"

"Yes; I was in St. Louis."

"Well, you ought to be getting work. You ought to be ashamed of yourself. Why, when Washington was your age he was a surveyor!"

"Well, when Washington was your age he was dead."

"I just happened to think—"

"I thought I heard something rattle."

"The other day I was standing in the kitchen of a house when a little mouse jumped out of the gas range."

"Well, what did you do?"

"I didn't do anything, although I had a gun."

"You had a gun? Then why didn't you shoot him?"

"I couldn't; he was out of my range."

"Where are you going?"

"Whose affair is that?"

"I just wanted to know, that's all. I couldn't tell from your dress whether it was to the opera or an operation."

CHARLES IRWIN AND KITTY HENRY

"It's horrid of you to run around saloons."

"I beg your pardon; you never saw me run around any saloon!"

"And your companions—they go to awful places."

"Yes, they go to places to which I wouldn't even take your mother."

"Aren't you awful to talk that way! Then, too, you promised me you would swear off drinking."

"I did."

"Really?"

"Yes, for weeks I went by one cafe after another without any hesitation. Then one night as I was going home I got to thinking how well I'd done—"

"Yes, go on."

"So I said, 'Well, just to show my appreciation of myself I'll buy myself a drink.' And I did."

"You say you've traveled?"

"Yes, I have been all over—every place."

"I know one place you haven't been."

"Where?"

"Heaven."

"Well, I meant places of more than 500 population."

———

"Do you know you're a beautiful girl? Every time I look into those dark brown eyes I'm intoxicated."

"Isn't that odd?"

"Yes, it must be your eye (high) balls."

———

BERT HANLON

I have just returned from abroad, where I visited all the capitals. In London they asked me what I was doing for the war. I of course said nothing. Over there I met the king, and we became inseparable. In fact, one almost never saw us together.

But the most charming fellow I met was an educated Chinese. His name was Hung Wun. I think his brother was hung, too. And although he was educated and charming, people talked about him. It wasn't that he was exactly dishonest, but you see he was born in a London fog and everything he touched was mist.

This chap and I wished to go to Paris and take a whirl at the gay life there. We had a thousand dollars between us. Yes, between us and Paris.

Finally, I took in Spain and Portugal, but I looked all around for the barber of Seville, but I couldn't find his shop.

Finally I went into Germany. Germany turns out some fine men. They got me in Hamburg. Hamburg is wonderful! One can find almost anything in hamburg. Just the other day at lunch I came across two buttons and the heel of an old rubber.

England is also a wonderful country. In England you can live a week on a guinea. But you can do that in Chicago, too.

KENNEY AND HOLLIS

"What are hiccoughs?"

"Why, I don't know."

"Messages from the departed spirits."

"How tall are you?"

"I'm six feet tall."

"How tall is your brother?"

"He's three feet tall."

"He's just half as tall as you, then?"

"Yes, he's only my half brother."

"We had a thief in our family."

"Is that so?"

"Yes, he was born on a foggy night."

"Well, what's that got to do with it?"

"Everything was mist."

CLARK AND VERDI

"What is your name?"

"Tony Cirofici Gonazeles Parique Pasquale Boots."

"Too long. I call you Tony Boots. Now answer these questions: What did your father do?"

"He was a shoemaker."

"After he was married to your mother you had all the shoes you wanted?"

"No, only boots."

"When you left the old country, how did you come —first or second class?"

"I came sewerage."

"How many years have you?"

"Two."

"No, I didn't mean ears to hear with—how old are you?"

"O, 50."

"How tall are you?"

"Half past five."

" You mean 5 feet 6 inches."

" Yes, yes; that's it."

" Very well, Tony Boots, I get you fine job."

" What?"

" I get you job manicuring streets."

" I got lots ambeesh."

" You work eight hours a day."

" Fine. I got lots ambeesh."

" All right. You can work ten hours a day instead."

———

MAYBELLE LEWIS AND PAUL McCARTHY

" I had an operation yesterday."

" You did!"

" The doctor took ten bones out of my hand."

———

" Don't you like me?"

" Yes, before Christmas."

" You haven't kissed me tonight."

" I know. Your mother's been hanging around and I'm afraid she wouldn't like it."

" Well, she wouldn't get it."

" Why do you always wear a high hat when spooning?"

" O, that's my spark plug."

" Silly! But seeing this is your birthday, I won't pay any attention. I've brought you a present. It's for your head."

" Hair oil?"

" No, a vacuum cleaner."

HARRY GREEN & CO.

"My name is George Washington Cohan, remember the cherry tree."

"Where did you work last?"

"In one of the stores of the International Cigar Store."

"Why aren't you working now?"

"I got fired for telling the truth."

"How's that?"

"A man came in and said, 'Give me a good cigar,' and I said to him 'I can't do it. We don't carry any good cigars.'"

"Well, doesn't that discourage you?"

"No, I expect to be president of the United States some day."

"Now, seriously, you don't expect that?"

"Why not? They're mighty careless who they pick for president these days."

"Well, I like your honesty. I'll pay you ten thousand dollars a year just to stay in my house and tell the truth."

"I'd like to take it, but I'm afraid I'd have to give it up. You couldn't stand the truth."

"You better take it."

"All right. Ten thousand a year—that's $30.50 a day, $2.50 an hour, 4 cents a minute. Gosh, I've made 8 cents just talking about it!" (Butler enters.)

"Your bawth is ready, sir."

"My what?"

"Your bawth. Don't you know—where you wash?"

"O, you mean the sink."

"I thought you said this man who was in love with my wife was a broker?"

"He is. I don't know anybody broker than he is."

RUCKER AND WINIFRED

"Now, this railroad we are going to build—"

"What, are you going to build a railroad?"

"Of course; haven't you heard of it yet?"

"No."

"Well, we're going to build a railroad through a mountainous territory. It will benefit the farmers a great deal throughout the country."

"How so?"

"Well, how long does it take a farmer to carry his produce to market at present?"

"With a mule it takes four days."

"There you are. When the new railroad is in operation, the farmer will be able to take his produce to market and return home the same day."

"That will be fine; but what will they do with the other three days?"

THE LEIGHTONS

"Do you have long working hours?"

"Yes, I work sixteen hours a day."

"You ought to belong to a union and then you'd only have to work eight hours a day."

"I do belong."

"But you say you work sixteen hours?"

"I belong to two unions."

"Well, you'd better go on the road with our show. You won't have a thing to do, no hard work at all."

"That sounds good."

"In fact, the hardest job you'll have will be to collect your salary."

"Do you think

I'm good looking enough to go with a show?"

"Certainly, you have a splendid set of teeth."

"I ought to. I've missed a lot of meals."

"I'll start you at $8 a week and raise you to $7 if you do your work well."

"Which is the most?"

"Why, $8 is more, of course, and $7 is less. But the less it is the more chance you have of getting it."

ALLEN AND HOWARD

"It's pretty hot, isn't it?"

"What's pretty about it?"

"Still, it's a nice little town."

"Yes, Cook and Peary have nothing on you."

"Why?"

"Discovering 'burghs.'"

"It's a prohibition town, too."

"Good night, town."

"It's named Ellsburg."

"They forgot to put on the H."

"Tomorrow's a big day here."

"Twenty-four hours long, eh?"

"Do you like tea?"

"I like the color of it."

"Maybe you'll try some wheat bread that mother made?"

"No, I prefer rye."

"But that's so heavy."

"Put a little rock in it."

RALPH HERZ

Some time ago when I went into the movies the director had some doubts as to my ability. To prove that I was an actor I started reciting: "To be, or not to be, that is the question—"

"Cut that!" shouted the director. "That isn't the question at all. The question is: How long can you stay under water?"

Yes, I'm working in pictures now. I am in a new feature. "Bringing Home Father," in three reels.

Most comedians at some time or another express a desire to play "Hamlet." I am one of the exceptions. Never can I remember when I wanted to play "Hamlet." I played Oshkosh, and that was hamlet enough for me.

ANDREW TOMBES AND BAIL LYNN, IN "THE BRIDE SHOP"

" Have you traveled far? "

" Sure. Look at the mud on my shoes. I understand you are something of a linguist."

" Yes, I speak several languages."

" Well, why don't you speak one of them? "

" All right, Ohio."

" That's no language; that's a state."

" No, that's Chinese for good morning."

" All right, it's my turn now—Philadelphia."

" Well, what does that mean? "

" That's American for 'Good-night.'"

" What have you got there? "

" I have here the woman's national dress."

" What is it? "

" It's a nightgown."

" But why national? "

" It covers a multitude of shins."

" I am connected with royalty."

" Is that so? "

"Yes, my mother was stung by a queen bee."

"I notice you've had your hair cut. What's your barber's name?"

"You like his work, eh?"

"No, I want to warn my friends against him."

OLIVER DRISCO

Well, well, this is the life. I'd much rather be doing this kind of stuff than teaching a bunch of kids at Sunday school. But that's my regular profession— Sunday school teaching. Some funny little incidents occur at a Sunday school. One Sunday morning a small boy, a child about four, came up to me and said: "Teacher, we've got a new baby at our house."

Not recognizing the child, I asked him: "Who are you?"

"O, I'm the old one," was his reply.

I love children. That's the reason I'm going to be married. You didn't know that before, did you? Well, it's a fact. I have given the matter serious considera- tion. I've been to four fortune tellers, two clairvoy- ants, looked through six sign books, dreamed on a lock of his hair, and I've been to three of these astrologers, and I've also been to a meejum, and they all say go ahead. You know I ain't one of these women who marry reckless.

As I was saying before, I used to be a Sunday school teacher. Now one would think that a Sunday school teacher is an old maid, but I'm not. I'm a widow with two children. Although I've been married twice, I'm about to go into it again. So this morning, while I was sitting at the breakfast table with my two children I told them I had something important to tell them. "What is it?" asked Willie. "Well, it is this. On Friday evening I shall marry Mr. Black." Well, there was a solemn pause for a moment and then little Willie asked earnestly: "Mother, when are you going to tell Mr. Black?"

———

EDDIE CLARKE

I'm not a tramp. I'm a lily. I toil not, neither do I spin. And Solomon in all his glory was not arrayed like me. The other day I asked a woman for something to eat. She said she hadn't a thing in the house to give me, and besides she was busy, as she had a couple of letters to write. I said: "Madame, let me lick the stamps. I can't starve."

She said: "What's the matter with your coat?" I said, "Insomnia. It hasn't had a nap in ten years." "Well," she said, "I'll give you a dipperful of water." I said, "Is that all you can give?" She said, "No, you can have as many dipperfuls as you want." Then she asked me what I thought of the scheme of free baths. I said, "They won't get none from me. No man is goin' to get me to bathe without payin' me for it."

Then I went to another house and rang the front door bell. The woman came to the door and I said, "Won't you help a poor man that lost all his friends in the Jacksonville fire?" "Why," she said, "you are the man that lost his family in the Galveston flood and was in the Charleston earthquake." I said, "I know it, mum, I'm one of the most unfortunate gentlemen on the face of the earth." "Well," she said, " I'll tell you where you can find a job sawing five cords of wood." "Where?" said I. "Around the corner of the next street," said she. "I'm much obliged to you," said I. "I might have run into it, if it hadn't been for you."

THE SHARROCKS

"C'mon, c'mon, show a little speed. It's gettin' so that whenever you walk it looks like your feet were about to take root and grow in the ground. (Buckling up her dress while she is squirming.) Say, what kind of a dance is this? Are you one-stepping or fox-trotting? If you gotta do a dance while I hook you up, hesitate. Women are a wise

bunch, believe me. Here you can't even dress yourselves and you want to vote."

"Well, I'm gettin' tired of going along from day to day without hittin' the grub wagon regular."

"Say, you et this mornin', didn't you? Didn't I blow you to coffee and?"

"Yes, you blew me to coffee and sinkers."

"Sinkers? What's sinkers?"

"Say, you oughta know what sinkers is. You lived on 'em all last winter."

DUNLAP AND BIRDEN

"I cannot wait any longer. I must take a kiss from you."

"I've never been kissed before, and I wouldn't want any one to think I've been kissed."

"But I won't tell a living soul."

"Well, if that's the case, I suppose I will have to."

"Um! That was good."

"Of course it was."

"And do the poor indulge in that way?"

"Quite frequently, my little dear; quite frequently."

"Well, well, well; and do they experience the same sensation as we do?"

"Absolutely."

"Well, let me tell you it's much too good for the working classes."

"I hear you were out on a party?"

"Yes, I and the orchestra leader. Believe me, he knows something else besides music. Sharps—"

"Yes?"

"And flats! My land, the flats that man knows! I will now sing a song about conductors and motormen, in fact, an opera."

"What do you call it?"

"Carmen."

BURLEY AND BURLEY

"I want you to do me a favor, Mac."

"How much?"

"I am going to make a speech at the club. What would you advise me to talk about?"

"About a minute."

"Have you ever spoken in public, Mac?"

"Sure."

"What did you say?"

"Not guilty."

"I want to talk about something original, out of my own head."

"Talk about a vacuum."

"Here is a conundrum. What is it you eat on, sleep on, and brush your teeth with?"

"I don't know. What is it you eat on, sleep on, and brush your teeth with?"

"A chair, a bed, and a tooth brush."

"I have a conundrum. Why is a woman like dough?"

"What's the answer?"

"Because a man needs her."

"That's a well bred one, isn't it? But you gave the wrong answer. A woman is like dough because it's hard to get off your hands. Now answer me this one."

"Go ahead."

"Is that a mustache on your lip or a splash from an auto?"

FRANK MILTON AND DE LONG SISTERS

"Hello, girls, what's your names?"

"We're the Hook & Eye team. I'm Miss Hook and she's Miss Eye."

"Well, well, how did you ever get together? We had a good act last week, the Veil sisters."

"The Veil sisters?"

"Yes, Dotty and Nettie."

McKAY AND ARDINE

"I shall now sing a very sad little song entitled, 'O, Give Me Just One Little Heart,' written by a fellow trying to make a flush. He drew a spade and had to go to work.

"I will then offer for your approval a brand new song called 'The Old Wooden Rocker.' I made that out of my own head and had enough left over to make a kitchen table."

JACK HENRY, ROSE GARDNER AND JOS. B. ROBERTS, IN "THE BACHELOR DINNER"

"You'd better laugh before you get married."

"Why?"

"Because you don't get a chance afterward."

"You don't say so."

"It's the truth. Do you know that father only laughed once after he married mother?"

"When was that?"

"When she caught her tongue in the wringer."

HOMER B. MASON AND MARGUERITE KEELER

"Where shall we go on our honeymoon?"

"Let's go to Niagara Falls."

"Is that place still running?"

HAMILTON AND BARNES

"What do you do for a living?"

"O, I have a flock of trained mosquitoes."

"Trained mosquitoes?"

"Exactly. One of them, Little Mike, is exceptionally clever. He's like Rockefeller."

"What do you mean?"

"He'll sting you in the end."

"O, let me see him."

"I can't; he's insane."

"Little Mike—insane? No."

"Yes."

"But how?"

"It's this way. One mosquito lives on a hazel nut, one lives on a pecan, one on a nigger toe, and—"

" Yes, yes; go on."

" And Little Mike always slept on an almond, and last night, last night he— "

" O!"

" He went off his nut."

" I suppose your livelihood will be impaired now?"

" O, no, I am an aviator."

" You fly?"

" Yes, I fly."

" I remember now—I saw your picture in the fly-paper!"

" O, you tickle me."

" What?"

" I say you tickle me."

" Aw, you tickle me first."

———

" Do you know anything about surgery?"
" O, yes; I shave myself."

———

" What does your father do?"

" Father is a traveling man."

" I'll bet your mother's jealous of him."

" She is; father is in wrong for life."

" No!"

" Yes. It happened thus: Father was going from Chicago to St. Paul and he found that the sleeper was crowded and thought himself lucky to have a berth. In the car was a poor old lady almost 80. Father never could see a lady stand, so he gave up his sleeping car bed to her, intending to take the next train."

" Well, what was there in that to make a wife jealous?"

"Why, then he went out and sent this telegram to his wife: 'Won't be home until later; gave berth to an old lady.'"

———

"Have you ever seen any races?"

"Many of them."

"What was the closest race you ever saw?"

"The Scotch."

———

MACK AND WALKER

"I wish the Lord had made me a man."

"He did; I'm the man."

———

"When I and another girl went abroad we traveled by steamer. I spent the whole of my first day in my berth."

"O, it was your birthday?"

"No, I never had a birthday."

"And you've had so many opportunities, haven't you?"

"I do wish you could meet my sister. She's tall and awfully good looking—not a bit like me."

"No fishing on these premises."

GEORGE QUIGLEY AND EDDIE FITZGERALD

" Don't try to flirt with every girl you meet. Beauty is only skin deep."

" Well, I'm no cannibal."

" Now, smile."

" Hahaha."

" Not so loud."

" Why not? This is no secret."

" As you have stood on a corner looking at a big, fine automobile speeding along at forty miles an hour, did you ever stop to think— "

" Yes, I did once, and I was in a hospital for six months."

" There comes your friend Kelly down the street. He just passed that saloon."

" Did he pass the saloon? "

" Yes."

" Well, it's not Kelly."

" Are you in favor of municipal ownership of public utilities? "

" I don't know him, but if he's a good Democrat I'll vote for him."

WALTER BROWER

I met my wife in a cabaret. She was a singer. I used to watch her as she'd go through the audience— not all of them, but most of them. It was funny how that girl couldn't hold on to her money. She simply couldn't keep it. Except on birthdays. Then I'd give her a dime or so. She was a sweet girl, but her father and I didn't get along well at all. He wanted me to work. I thought I had better move, so we moved the next week. It was terribly simple. I didn't have to carry a thing, not even a suitcase. I had the ticket for it, though.

After we got out we decided to take a taxi but my wife only had a dime, so we took a street car instead. The car was terribly crowded. I was breaking in a pair of shoes for a friend and my feet hurt terribly.

I'll never forget the time we were married. She came into the room leaning on her father's arm and two friends held me up. She was dressed in a princess slip and I was afraid every moment that it would. Her brother did not appear at the ceremony. I was dressed in a brown suit that didn't fit me very well. That was why the brother was not present. The best man wore a regular evening suit, and everybody thought he was the lucky one. He was, but I didn't realize it at the time.

In truth, I must say the bride was the ugliest I have ever seen. Her mother must have thought an awful lot of children to bring her up. The bridesmaids wore Helen pink. I had better say, "were."

At last we reached the end of the aisle. The gentleman beamed down on me and said: "Young man, have you ever been arrested before and . . . " No, no. I was wrong. That was another time.

After the ceremony was through I asked him what the charge was. He told me that it was not the custom to charge a fixed price, but that usually the groom gave the minister whatever the ceremony was worth to him. I gave him a dime. He gave me back a nickel.

McINTYRE AND HEATH,
IN "THE GEORGIA MINSTRELS"

"Well, here we are."

"Yes, and we're going to stay here—broke. But if I ever get back to my livery stable again you bet I'll make love to that job."

"What you complaining 'bout, Alexander? How long you been with the troupe?"

"Four days."

"Well, you got the base drum for your services, didn't you?"

"Yes, but that ain't eating."

"Do you remember, Alexander, that great joke of yours that you told me first in the liberty stable? That joke that went like this: 'Why is the heart of a tree like a dog's tail?' And the answer was: 'Because it's a long way from the bark.' Do you remember that joke, Alexander?"

"Do I remember, Henry? That was the joke that took me away from home. That was the joke that you said would make me famous. You told me I was talented, a great comedian, a great funny man."

"And so you were, Alexander. You were the funniest specimen I ever did see. And didn't I discover you in a liberty stable and promise you a future?"

"That's what you did. You told me we would travel in high class trains and all I would have to do would be to sit at the window and watch the lambs gamboling in the fields."

"Yes, yes, Alexander."

"And, doggone it, you know there wasn't a window

in any of the cars we traveled on. You told me, too, that we would eat at swell hotels, and you had me practisin' how to eat with a fork for four days, and—"

"How long is it since you've had anything to eat, Alexander?"

"I forget."

"You forget, Alexander! To me it is the memory of the last meal that keeps me alive."

"And listen to me, Henry. If I ever get back to my livery stable job the first man that tells me I've got talent is never goin' to tell me again. And I have got a letter from my wife, too. She has left me."

"How much?"

"It isn't that kind of a left. She wrote me for money and I told her I didn't have any, but sent her my love and inclosed a check for 1,000 kisses. Now read this letter."

"'Dear Alexander: The iceman has cashed your check.'

"So, Henry, I haven't any more home than a rabbit."

———

HARRY COOPER AND ROSS ROBERTSON, IN "THE MAIL CARRIER"

Cooper—When I fell out of the auto I landed on my head.

Robertson—Weren't you hurt?

Cooper—Where there is no sense there is no feeling.

Robertson—How would you like to own a flivver?

Cooper—I'd rather own an automobile.

Robertson—I know where you can get two flivvers cheap.

Cooper—Thanks, I don't need a pair of skates.

Ross — I've been working long enough. I want to retire.

Harry—Why don't you go to bed?

Ross—In your new job you have a chance to make $5,000.

Harry—Five thousand dollars? Why, that's a Halsted street million.

Ross—What is your name?

Harry — Isaac Fitzpatrick Cohen.

Ross — Why the Fitzpatrick?

Harry—That's for protection.

Ross — In what state were you born?

Harry—I'm not sure.

Ross—Come, come. You surely know in what state you were born.

Harry—I know; naked.

Ross—How tall are you?

Harry—Five feet eleven, but you can have it for five feet nine.

Ross—Are you married?

Harry—Yes, but the expression on my face comes from cramps. Here's a picture of my wife.

Ross—Why, that's a picture of Lillian Russell!

Harry—Well, my wife looks just like that if you cover up her face.

Ross—How do you like married life?

Harry—Oh, it's too expensive. It's pretty tough when a man pays 30 cents a pound for a steak.

Ross—Yes.

Harry—And when you pay only 15 it's tougher.

Ross—How much does your wife weigh?

Harry—Three hundred and sixty-five pounds—just two pounds lighter than our horse.

Ross—Does she eat very much?

Harry—Oh, not very much. Why, in the morning all she has is a small eight-pound steak smothered with lamb chops.

Ross—Have you got a family?

Harry—Shuah I got a family. I got all my wife's relatives.

Ross—Any children?

Harry—One.

Ross—Boy or girl?

Harry—Musician.

Ross—But it must be a boy or a girl? Which is it?

Harry—Both.

Ross—But how can it be both?

Harry—Because it is twins.

What is the difference between a Ford and an automobile?

I know; an automobile can't climb a tree.

ROBINSON AND NICHOLS

"Whenever the weather looks rainy I eat a salt herring."

"Why?"

"That keeps me dry."

"Who was that elderly man you were talking to a few minutes ago?"

"That was my father."

"How aristocratic he looks with all that gray hair."

"Yes, and he's got me to thank for it."

"I love you."

"I've heard that before."

"I worship you madly."

"Loose talk."

"I cannot live without your love."

"Get some new stuff."

"Will you marry me?"

"Well, now, there's some class to that."

"Why is a mother-in-law like dough?"

"I don't know."

"Because she's so hard to get off one's hands."

"Is anybody taking you out to dinner tonight?"

"No."

"You'll be awful hungry tomorrow."

"How often do you shave?"

"Three times a week every day but Sunday, then I shave every day."

"Will you embark with me on the ocean of matrimony?"

"I'm afraid I might get seasick."

"When a man pays attention to a woman it is generally a sign that he wishes to marry her."

"And when a man doesn't pay attention to a woman it is generally a sign that he has married her."

"Will you love me always?"

"Passionately, my darling."

"And you'll never cease to love me?"

"Never, my darling."

"And will you save your money?"

"Every penny."

"And you'll never speak harshly to me?"

"Never."

"And you'll get along with mamma and papa, and do just what mamma wants you to do?"

"Yes."

"And just what papa wants you to do?"

"Yes."

"And just what I want you to do?"

"Of course."

"Well, I will be yours; but I fear I am making an awful mistake."

"What is a flirtation?"

"Attention without intention."

"Would you be willing to work for a husband?"

"Yes, until I had him."

"I like to kiss a sassy girl."

"Why?"

"Because she always gives me 'plenty of lip.'"

JOS. E. HOWARD AND ETHELYN CLARK

"I would like to marry you, if you have no objections."

"Well, none that I can think of at present."

"Would you scream for help if I should kiss you?"

"Would you need help?"

FREAR AND BAGGOTT

"To look at me you wouldn't think that I was a very smart man, would you?"

"Well, not above the ordinary, no."

"No, but I came from a smart family; I've got a brother that's a miracle."

"How is that?"

"He lives in two countries at the same time."

"Explain yourself."

"The other day I got a letter from London, England. This is what he said: 'Dear brother: Here I am in London, England, and I am home sick.'"

"Do you know Mr. Hook?"

"Hook and I are old associates."

"Do you know anything about music?"

"You can't fool me on music; I know every bar from the Battery to One Hundred and Twenty-fifth street."

"Say, Jim, what was the Delaware river a hundred years ago?"

"Go 'long, you fool; it was a river, of course."

"No, it wasn't; it was a bottle of ink."

"How do you make that out?"

"Because it was no good till there was a Penn in it."

KNAPP AND CORNALLA

"I'm a great bear hunter."

"Tell me of a few narrow escapes you've had from bears."

"Young man, if there's been any narrow escapes it's the bears that had them, not me."

"Interesting!"

"I own a hunting dog that never misses a trail once he gets on it."

"Keen after a scent, eh?"

"Yes; he used to belong to John D. Rockefeller. I guess that's the reason."

"Without any exaggeration I can say that living in this town is heaven on earth."

"You don't tell me!"

"Why, yes. We have hundreds of people in this town who wouldn't leave it under any circumstances."

"What cemetery are they buried in?"

"This is also a great country for hogs."

"I noticed that while riding on a trolley car. One man wouldn't give a stout old lady his seat."

"Let her stand on her feet, eh?"

"No; let her stand on my feet."

"And I mustn't forget to tell you this town is also a great railroad center. Fifty trains pass through here every day."

"That's fine."

"But none of them stop."

PIPIFAX AND PANLO

"A hobo just sold me this police whistle for a nickel. I'll blow it and see if it's any good. (Blows whistle.) Yes, the whistle is good, all right."

"Did you ring?"

"Bless my heart, if it ain't my old friend McGinty!"

"Officer McGinty, if you please."

"I didn't know you were a policeman."

"O, yes, a regular policeman."

"I can't believe it."

"Have you change for $10?"

"Why, yes."

"Give me that! How dare you have money?"

AVON COMEDY FOUR

"How much does the doctor charge for a visit?"

"Five dollars for the first visit and $3 for the second."

"Hello, doctor, here I am again."

"What do you smoke?"

"I smoke stogies. My brother smokes fish."

"How much coffee do you drink?"

"About twelve saucers full."

"Why don't you drink it out of a cup?"

"I can't. The spoon always hits me in the nose."

"Keep your mouth open and say fish."

"Herring."

"Aren't you going to pay me for my advice?"

"No; I'm not going to take it."

MARIE FITZGIBBON

A little girl was in the habit of praying every night. One night, after asking for a blessing for her father and mother and her many little brothers and sisters, she added: "And please God don't send father any more children. He doesn't treat the ones he's got now right at all."

A teacher in a public school asked her class of little tots to stand at the blackboard and draw the picture of what they wanted when they grew up. All the class but one responded. This one was a little boy.

"Willie," said the teacher, "don't you want to be anything at all?"

"Yessum," said Willie, "I want to be married, but I don't know how to draw it."

On another day she asked the pupils to state what they had to thank God for. One little girl said she thanked him for her pretty rosy cheeks, another for her long hair, and a husky youngster volunteered his gratitude to the Creator because he was a good baseball player. Only one boy refused to say anything. He was freckled, bowlegged, and all his teeth were missing.

"Thomas," said the teacher, encouragingly, "haven't you got anything to thank God for?"

"Naw," the youngster said, "he darned near ruined me."

ROSIE LLOYD

Last week I waved my handkerchief at one man for three hours. And then I found out I had been flirting with a scarecrow. I was married once—just once.

That was plenty. I met my husband by the pale moon, we got married by the full moon, and I lost him on our honeymoon.

We lived together for fifteen years. In all those fifteen years there never was a fight in our house. But we had a fine back yard. Hard drink finally killed him. He choked on a piece of ice.

Sometimes I feel lonely, so to while away the hours I've been saving tobacco coupons. For three thousand coupons I can get either a husband or a carpet sweeper.

I think I'll take a husband, because I can wipe up the floor with him instead.

Men put on airs because they were created first. But they shouldn't. Ain't first experiments always failures? Then again, woman has been accused of making a fool out of man. Well, if she did she found her task half completed before she ever began.

Some maids consider a husband necessary to their happiness. But let me tell you one thing, girls. If any of you should get disappointed in lassoing some poor prune here's a good substitute. Get a dog that growls all morning, a parrot that swears all afternoon, and a cat that stays out all night and you'll know exactly what married life is.

FROM "SO LONG LETTY"

" I don't see how any woman could help loving you."
" I don't give them any help—they do it anyway."

" He gave you a nasty look."
" I know it."
" Yes, Letty; a nasty look."
" Have I still got it?"

" You should eat onions. They build you up physically."
" Yes, but they pull you down socially."

" There you go smoking again! I'll bet when I'm not around to watch you that you just smoke one cigar after another."

"That's the way to smoke 'em—one after another. There's something I want to criticise you about, too. You should read more. It broadens you."

"I'm broad enough already."

———

"Where are your husbands?"

"O they're traveling men."

"So?"

"Yes, they are home every Monday between 2 and 4."

———

"Please won't you stop drinking for your wife's sake?"

"I'm not drinking for your wife's sake."

———

WHIPPLE AND HUSTON

"Did you ever have money left you?"

"Yes, I had money—and it left me quick."

"Well, I have money—lots of it—a million."

"Will you marry me?"

"I should say not!"

"O, very well. I just wanted to know how it felt to lose a million."

———

"Are you talented?"

"Yes, I paint."

"Did you ever paint a natural picture?"

"Indeed, I painted a picture so natural that the barber came to shave it three times a week."

FROM "THE HIGHEST BIDDER"

"When a man marries he expects to be plastered with two or three relatives—that's history. And relatives often mean the divorce route. But, anyway, I never touched you in any but an affectionate way, did I?"

"You held my wrists that night."

"Yes, but that was in self-defense."

"Anyway, in my divorce bill I have stated that you have an earning capacity of $150 a week."

"Does the bill state that?"

"In black and white."

"Now, that's funny; I've been trying to make the firm believe that same thing for two years."

WILL ROGERS

Ziegfeld has a way of dressing a chorus girl so that you don't know whether she has or whether she hasn't; and you go away and wonder about it two or three days, and then you come back to have another look.

They say that a shark won't bite at a leg that has a stocking on it. These theatregoers must think they're sharks, the way they strain their eyes to determine whether they're being worn or not.

The ladies say that getting a job with a Ziegfeld show is largely a matter of form. Then how did William Rock's crooked shanks get into the Follies? He has the lumpiest knees I ever saw; I wouldn't be the first to knock 'em, but they knock each other.

And Rock's partner, Miss White, is a peach. If I could work with her, I'd be willing to look like Rock.

The girls of the Frolic wear a little less each year. I only ask that my life be spared until I see three more Frolics.

Every time I see one of these shows I go out and put a dollar and a tear of sympathy in a blind man's cup.

Well, the summer is about over, and what will these butterflies do then? Some of these girls don't know where their next limousine is coming from.

People think I can't be a real cowboy, or I wouldn't work in a show where there's nothing but calves.

One fellow in the audience said he could do things with a rope that I couldn't do. I confessed that he was right when I saw him lighting a Pittsburgh stogie. He could smoke a rope, and I can't.

So many exciting things have happened this summer that people haven't had time to laugh at the Palm Beach suits. When a fellow puts across something funny, he ought to get a laugh; and those little half-hearted belts and ruffles are as good as anything Charlie Chaplin ever pulled. Wouldn't those suits be just as cool if they fit?

Well, Germany got her submarine back, Shackleton

got his Polar party back, and if the Giants get back without losing their uniforms we'll all be happy.

It begins to look like Brooklyn. Colonel Ebbets may have to make another speech. Once at a banquet he said: "Baseball has grown and grown until now it is in its infancy!"

Roosevelt said: "I'm out of politics. I'll be found in the Hughes camp."

Hughes said: "I'm for America first." After the way America has kept him in office all his life, we didn't expect he'd come out for Venezuela!

Bryan said: "Every day the war is nearer its close." And yet he wonders why he never could be elected President.

The Erie Railroad claims it can't run trains on the eight-hour-day plan. They say that if they mustn't run a train more than eight hours at a shift they'll have to put the stations closer together all along their lines.

The boys that are back from the Mexican border say the reports were wrong that said it was 115 in the shade down there. There wasn't any shade.

They say the Mexican soldiers fight without making any trenches. That's right. Unless the Mexicans have changed a lot since I knew them, they'd rather be shot than go to work and dig a trench.

The Mexican soldiers get 10 cents a day for serving in the army. And the only day they earn it is the day they try to collect it.

The Mexicans eat so much chili pepper that when they're killed the coyote can't eat their bodies. But if Uncle Sam ever has to pepper them with his machine guns there won't be a big enough piece left to burn a buzzard's mouth.

MOSS AND ERY

"Was that fair down at your club a success?"

"Pretty near; but not exactly a success."

"Why wasn't it?"

"Four men managed to escape with their carfare."

———

"I am really beginning to believe that Margaret has a soft spot in her heart for me."

"What makes you think that?"

"Why, the dear girl says she is always thinking of me."

"That's nothing to go by. A woman doesn't think with her heart. In all probability the soft spot you mention is in her head."

———

"Where are you going?"

"To buy a wedding present."

"A wedding present?"

"Yes; my son is getting murdered."

"Your son is getting what?"

"Murdered, murdered."

"Not murdered; you mean to say married."

"What's the difference?"

———

CARL McCULLOUGH

I was watching Hiram packing for a trip to Europe and noticed that he put a woman's night gown in his trunk. "What's that for?" I asked.

"That's to wear on the ship," said Hiram. "In case of a wreck it's women and children first."

Hiram was on a train one day when the sheriff got on with a lunatic, who was handcuffed. They sat in front of Hiram and after a while he leaned over to the sheriff and said: "What's the matter with him?"

"Bugs," said the sheriff.

"Bugs?" asked Hiram.

"Yes, bugs in his head. He's insane."

"Well," said Hiram, "with bugs in his head and handcuffed, I should think he would be."

HARRY FERN AND COMPANY

"Say, this apple isn't good. It's full of worms."

"O, that doesn't make any difference."

"It certainly does."

"O, no, the apple is full of worms and the worm is full of apple, so if you bite right ahead you are bound to get what you want."

"What is your business?"

"I'm in the mining business."

"Gold and silver mining?"

"No, calcimining."

"I have paid the rent for four years and owed for three. That makes it forty-three years."

"Where's the superintendent of that institution over yonder?"

"O, no one ever sees him."

"Hasn't he any friends?"

"Friends! Say, that man has fewer friends than an alarm clock."

LOUIS MADDEN AND COMPANY

"Yes, I spent the summer at one of those beach resorts. After I had laid in my bed three hours I got up covered with stone bruises. That's the kind of a hotel it was."

"Did you have a good time bathing?"

"O, the tide was out most of the time, but when it came in we had a real good swim."

"I suppose you met some of the girls?"

"Yes, I fell for a rich girl. Her father followed the horses, and . . . "

"I suppose he drove a horse car, eh?"

"Certainly not. She was a fine girl. She was one

of those girls who don't know anything about makeup —and you know how scarce they are these days."

"Well, what was the trouble?"

"She was way beyond me. Just imagine her marrying a vaudeville actor. You know I never got any better than third on the bill, and you know what that would mean; she and her rich parents would be just starting on their soup when I was finishing my act."

SOPHIE AND HARVEY EVERETT

"I was out to see your brother at the insane asylum today."

"What did he have to say?"

"O, he's crazy to see you."

"How many make a million?"

"Very few."

"I've got a horse that can go to beat the band."

"Then the band must be on foot."

"I hear you were in a fight today."

"I had a fight, but I wasn't in it."

"You say your mother has the mumps; you want to look out—mumps are contagious."

"She's my stepmother—she wouldn't give me anything."

"The man who was run over by the cars the other day is now out of danger."

"That's good."

"He died this morning."

"My, that is a swell suit. You're a credit to your tailor."

"You're wrong. Now that I've got the suit I'm a debit to my tailor."

"I see they're getting airships down pretty fine."

"Yes, but they're still having lots of trouble getting them up."

"Why doesn't your brother get his hair cut?"

"Shear fright, I guess."

"What is next to an oyster?"

"The shell."

"I have a suit of clothes for every day in the week."

"Where are they?"

"This is it I have on."

"Chicago is a beautiful city. Would you believe it, today was the first time I ever saw a patrol wagon."

"How did you like it?"

"Why, I was carried away with it."

"What is the difference between an elephant and a mosquito?"

"What is the difference?"

"The shape."

"How did you lose your hair?"

"Worry."

"What did you worry about?"

"About losing my hair."

"Did you ever take a bicycle trip?"

"Once."

"Where did you go?"

"Straight over on my neck."

MORTON AND MOORE

"What'll you have to eat?"

"Three boiled eggs."

"Yes, sir."

"And listen."

"Yes, sir."

"One of them must be good."

"Say, I'd be ashamed if I had a bald head like yours. Look at my head of hair."

"I just want to ask you one question."

"Well, what is it?"

"Did you ever see grass growing on a busy street?"

"I saw a thrilling chase recently."

"Tell me."

"I saw a sheriff's posse chase a bandit. The bandit fled into the hills and crawled into a cave. The sheriff tried his hardest to get him out. But that bandit stayed in there seven days. Think of it!"

"Impossible! He would have starved."

"O no, he drank milk."

" Milk! Where did he get milk? "

" He had the sheriff's goat."

———

" What's the matter with your face? Do you drink coffee? "

" No, I don't. I drink cocoa."

" Then there's something the matter with your cocoa."

———

MAY PAGE TAYLOR

I didn't sleep much all last night; in fact, I'm a very light sleeper. That is, I'm a woman who is easily awakened and is a long time getting to sleep. Well, anyhow, last night I slept in a hotel, and such a hotel it is. Why, I couldn't get to sleep at all. I tossed about that bed for about two hours. Then I finally succeeded in getting into a sound sleep. I was asleep for about fifteen minutes when I heard a loud knock on the door, so I yelled out. "What you want?" I said it just like that.

"Package downstairs for you, lady," came back the answer.

"Well, let it stay down there till morning," I shouted back.

The boy he shuffled down the corridor and after a long time I fell into a sound sleep again. I was asleep about twenty minutes this time when another knock came on the door. So I yelled out again: "What you want now?"

Then came back a slow reply: "That package."

"Yes," says I.

"Well, it ain't for you," shouted back the bellhop.

THE FARBER GIRLS

"Do you like to dance?"

"Yes, the boys say I'm awfully light on their feet."

"Do you like music?"

"Why, I know every bar from here to Hammond."

"Don't you think the Blue Danube is intoxicating?"

"Yes, but I can get mine just as quick on Green Mountain."

"I met a Johnnie last night."

"Did you make a hit?"

"I should say so! He'd get down on his knees and die for me."

"But will he get up on his feet and work for you?"

———

"There are two things you can't disguise—a married man and a Ford."

"How can you tell?"

"By their clutch."

"Do you know artists are seeking me all the time to pose for them? Fisher has been after me for weeks, and—"

"Fisher!"

"No other. He's simply crazy about my profile."

"You mean to tell me that you're going to be model for the great Harrison Fisher?"

"No—Bud."

CRESSY AND DAYNE

"Liquor makes men do desperate things, doesn't it?"

"I should say so. It made me spend 50 cents to hear Bryan lecture."

"I don't see why you want to stay in the show business. What do you get out of it?"

"I got this car out of it."

"I mean something that's worth while."

"That will be all from you. At that, though, an automobile is a great deal like a man; it smokes and kicks and comes home at night lit up. By the way, what was the last show that played here?"

"'Ben Hur.'"

"Was it a success?"

"Yep, it kept me pretty busy sellin' tickets. There

was a line outside the theater, but they finally got in —both of 'em."

"Did the cast make a hit?"

"Yes, Ben he did pretty well, but the audience didn't seem to take to Hur."

JAMES B. CARSON, IN "THE RED HEADS"

"Give me some orders, will you?"

"Yes, I'll give you two right now."

"Well—"

"Get out and stay out."

COHAN AND YOUNG

"Well, how did you like riding in the subway?"

"It would be nice if there wasn't any lights."

"Now, don't be naughty."

"I don't like the conductors on those subway trains."

"Why, what's the matter with them?"

"When I was getting off from the train he shouted out to me, 'Wash your neck, wash your neck.'"

"The conductor told you to wash your neck?"

"Yes, he shouted out just like that, 'Wash your neck, wash your neck.'"

"The conductor didn't tell you to wash your neck; he was telling you to watch your step."

"Yes, just the same."

"Were there any nice girls in New York?"

"Sure. I got a fine New York girl."

"A fine, good looking girl, eh?"

"I don't know."

"You don't know if she's good looking or pretty?"

"No, but she's rich."

"I suppose you did some spooning with her?"

"O, yes; one night we sat in her parlor, the lights were out, she sat on my lap."

"She sat on your lap—then what did you sit on?"

"A pin her kid brother put on the chair."

"Did you come down hard on the pin?"

"Of course I came down hard. She was sitting on my lap at the time."

REED BROTHERS

"How fast have you ever traveled?"

"I have traveled at the rate of seventy miles an hour."

"That's nothing. I have traveled so fast that you couldn't see trees or telegraph poles."

"Why, how was that?"

"I was locked up in a boxcar."

"Say, I went up to a farmhouse the other day and asked for some cold victuals."

"Did you get any?"

"Yes, I got the cold shoulder."

"Say, your father was pretty wealthy when he died, wasn't he?"

"Oh, yes."

"Did he leave your mother much?"

"About twice a week."

"I fell down a hill with ten bottles of beer and didn't break one of them."

"How did you accomplish such a wonderful feat?"

"I had them inside of me."

"If you should die, what would you do with your body?"

"I don't know."

"I'd sell mine to a medical student."

"Then you'd be giving yourself dead away."

"I fell into a piece of property the other day."

"Get out."

"Yes; a fellow left a coal hole open

and I fell in it. But I sued the fellow."

"What did you get?"

"I got six months for stealing coal."

———

"Who were the first gamblers?"

"Adam and Eve."

"How so?"

"Didn't they shake a paradise?"

"They say that whisky has killed more men than bullets."

"Well, I'd sooner be full of whisky than bullets, wouldn't you?"

———

BILLY HALLIGAN AND DAMA SYKES

Billy—Have you ever been to Gary?

Dama—No; have you?

Billy—Oh, yes. I know the American consul there. It's a great town. They used to blow the curfew at 9 o'clock, but they had to stop it.

Dama—Why?

Billy—It woke everybody up.

Dama—What is your business?

Billy—Real estate. It's the greatest thing on earth. Mostly earth. I'm selling lots in Evanston. In fact, I sold property there to William Jennings Bryan and Dr. Cook, and a lot of others.

Dama—Did you try to sell President Wilson a lot?

Billy—Yes.

Dama—What did he say?

Billy—He said he'd make a note of it.

Dama—Where is Evanston?

Billy—That's a suburb of Calvary. Buy a lot now. We take anything, cash, trading stamps or goldfish. Pay $100 down and 10 cents a month for the rest of your life. We give a pair of rubber boots with every lot. Ten cents from each purchase is donated toward the purchase of a new battleship for the United States.

Dama—What's the battleship for?

Billy—To go with the one we have.

Dama—You're a very good salesman.

Billy—Not as good as my brother. He's selling pretzels in London. But I want you to try one of our lots. It's only an hour's swim from the city.

Dama—Could you use $1,000?

Billy—Yes. That would just buy a club sandwich in the College Inn. Look at me. I am young and promising. I have a great future behind me. I never drop a drink.

Dama—What are your office hours?

Billy—From 12 to 1. I take an hour out for lunch.

Dama—What is a gondola?

Billy—A gondola is a Venetian jitney. **Did you**
ever hear of Fort Garlica?

Dama—No.

Billy—That's an Italian stronghold. Garlic is "**The**
Breath of a Nation." By the way, where were you
born?

Dama — I was
born in Detroit.

Billy—Oh, that's
where all those lit-
tle things come
from. It reminds
me of the peace
ship. The peace
ship went to Scan-
dinavia bearing this
motto, "Put It All
on One Check."

Dama — Where
were you born?

Billy—I was born
in Detroit, too. My
father was in the furniture business. His motto was
"Feather Your Nest." But he wanted too much down.

Billy—Tell me, my dear young lady, have you ever
been in South Haven in the summer?

Dama—Yes, and I just love it!

Billy—Ah, then we can speak freely. Speaking of
traveling, have you ever been in Portugal?

Dama—Where's Portugal?

Billy—That's where Gaby Deslys gave the **King
Manuel** training.

Billy—My face is my fortune.

Dama—That's what people say about mine, too.

Billy—Fine! Let's put our faces together.

———

STUART BARNES

It is wonderful to see a young man in love. One night a week he gets a bouquet of flowers and goes to

his girl's house. When he gets to the door his knees begin to wabble and when some one answers the ring he asks: "Is Miss Smith in?" Is she in? Why, for two hours she's been sitting looking out the window for the rubberhead to show up, and when he finally has arrived she sends some one else to let him in and say: "I'll see if she's in."

Then finally the poor goat is led into the front room and told to be seated, that Miss Smith will be down presently. And while Miss Smith is waiting for a sufficient time to elapse to give the lunkhead the idea that she is finishing her toilet all her little brothers and sisters pass by the door and gawk in at the big goof and make him more and more miserable. He's on view. He's sister's exhibit, and they all want a look at what she's caught.

Finally she comes and they talk; that is, she talks and he says, " O, yes." " Uh-huh." " Of course." She invites him to dinner because she wants pa and ma to get a close view of the poor fish, and he accepts.

He is so wabbly at the table that he puts butter on his salad and vinegar on his meat. Ma asks him if he will have tea or coffee and he answers, " A little of both." In trying to use his handkerchief he takes hold of the table cloth and upsets everything on the table. When he has calmed down dinner is over and he tells them what a lovely dinner he had and how much he enjoyed it.

Say what you will against women, statistics go to prove that half our parents have been women.

CHARLES OLCOTT

I have lots of fun watching a comic opera. After the opening chorus a cute little blonde steps out and says, " Here comes the king." She gets $2 more a week since she was raised from the chorus. Of course, she won't speak to the mere chorus girls.

Then there is a king and his lord of the exchequer. The king is thin and the exchequer is fat. After the show has been out three weeks the ex. is as thin as the king. The king in musical comedy has a beautiful daughter. The king wants her to marry Ferdinand, who is rich. She wants to marry Alphonso, who is

poor. The kings' daughters always love the poor ones
—in plays.

The princess tells the king: "I do not love Ferdinand. So!"

The king says: "Why do you not love Ferdinand
so?"

She says: "Because I love Alphonso."

The hero says to the king: "I must have the
damsel."

The king says: "Put him in the dungeon. There
he'll have a damp cell."

RITA GOULD

Dear old Boston. There's a city for you. You may
talk about New York till further orders, but for me
the big beanery on Massachusetts Bay. Give me the
home of John Stetson. Say, did you ever go to the
theater with anybody from Boston? You can take a
Boston man to see Bernhardt, Langtry, Rehan, Mar-
lowe or Adams and before the first act is over he'll say:
"She's good, but did you ever see Annie Clarke?"

But, say, did you ever kiss a Boston girl? No,
honest, did you? Now, you know if you kiss a New
York girl you're liable to melt the gold in your teeth.
The moment you grab her she wants to bite her name
in your neck.

And before you let go she says: "What time will
you be here tomorrow night?" But the Boston girl
straightens up until she feels as far above you as the
gilded dome on Beacon Hill and says as she wipes her
glasses: "Mr. Tremont, your conduct shocks me be-

yond all utterance." The other day I was coming along one of the principal cow paths in the village when a man asked me if I could tell him why the Boston Herald was like China.

I said, "No," and he said, "Because it's on the opposite side of the Globe." But did you ever notice the way they talk in Boston? Now, you know you'll hear a New York girl say: "What are you giving us, taffy?" A Boston girl never says that. She says: "Of what would you like to make me the recipient, a confection whose chief ingredient is molasses?"

CONLIN AND PARKS TRIO

"Are you married?"

"Yes, I'm a grass widow."

"You don't happen to need a nice lawn mower, do you?"

"O. S. O. S. S. O. S.!"

"What does S. O. S. mean?"

"Soused Over Sunday."

"Hey, mister, where are you going?"

"What's that to you? Get out of my way!"

"Won't you tell me what you're looking for?"

"Sure, I will, you boob. I'm looking for a fight."

"All right, I'll help you look for it."

"Say, what are all those names you have in that book?"

"Those are the names of the men I can lick."

"Well, what in blazes do you mean by having my name down there? You can't lick me."

"All right, I'll rub your name out."

"I can't eat peas. I simply can't eat peas."

"You can't? Why not?"

"They lie heavy on my stomach."

"Funny, they roll off of mine."

FRANK FOGARTY

"Dan Doyle died, and when they were carrying his corpse out of the house O'Brien came along and

said to Clancy, one of the pall bearers, 'What are you doing?' and Clancy said, 'Didn't you know Danny Doyle died? We are carrying him out now.' 'You don't mean it!' says O'Brien. 'Sure I mean it,' says Clancy. 'What did you think we were doing, rehearsing the funeral?'"

"Did you know that Kerrigan and O'Brien dropped dead at the same time at the hospital? It was like this: Kerrigan and O'Brien were talking together about their operations. Kerrigan says to O'Brien: 'The doctor sewed me up and left his scissors inside me.' O'Brien says to Kerrigan, 'The doctor left a spool of thread in me.' Just then the doctor came in and said, 'Has any one seen my satchel?' Kerrigan and O'Brien dropped dead."

"Mrs. Murphy and Mrs. Clancy live in the same house, Mrs. Murphy in the front and Mrs. Clancy in the rear. The other day Mrs. Murphy said to Mrs. Clancy, 'Did you know that the Russians dragged the czar's secretary through the streets?' 'No, I didn't,' replied Mrs. Clancy. 'That's what you get when you live in the rear. You don't see nothing.'"

HUFF AND CHAIN

"What smells worse than a goat?"

"Two goats."

"What is your brother?"

"A politician."

"Republican?"

"No."

"Democratic?"

"No."

"Then what are his principles?"

"He has none. Didn't you just hear me say he is a politician?"

"If it takes two yards of cloth to make a shirt, how many shirts can you get out of one yard?"

"It all depends on how dark the night is and how many shirts are on the line."

"How many children are there at your house?"

"Fourteen."

"You mean to say there are fourteen children at your house?"

"Yes; we got one and an Italian family that lives upstairs has thirteen."

DICK TRAVERS

One night I was sitting in a north side café with a party, one of whom—Henry we called him—did quite a little drinking. As the waiter passed us he called out to the chef, "One stew!" One of the party nudged Henry. "Somebody's paging you, Henry," he said.

BERNARD AND SHAW

"Where are you bound for?"

"I'm going to order a tombstone for my rich uncle who died last week."

"What did your uncle die of?"

"Malaria."

"There's only one thing will cure malaria—that's whisky and quinine."

"Where can you get it?"

"The whisky and quinine?"

"No, the malaria."

"I just saw you come out of a saloon."

"I was merely partaking of a little stimulant by the advice of my doctor."

"Who is your doctor?"

"I'm the doctor."

"Do you know that last year in this country over sixteen hundred million dollars was spent for liquor? That's terrible!"

"You're right. Something ought to be done to reduce the price of drink."

"Is there a single thing you can say in favor of liquor?"

"Yes, they say a glass of whisky will break up a cold."

"Yes, and six glasses will break up a home."

"I haven't got a home. I'm a widower."

"You ought to get married again."

"No, thanks; it's cheaper to have my socks darned at the laundry."

"How did you get your wife?"

"Through advertising."

"Then you'll admit that advertising pays?"

"I'll admit that it brings results."

"Perhaps you don't know that I'm a divorced woman."

"Indeed?"

"Yes, and I'm also an actress."

"You don't tell me."

"Half the managers on Broadway owe me money."

"Back salary or alimony?"

"Don't jest."

"Did your husband leave you much?"

"About twice a week."

"No, no! I mean did he leave any property?"

"Nothing but a pair of suspenders."

"O, well, they'll help support you."

MARIE SABBOTT AND ARMAND WRIGHT

"What are you all dressed up for?"

"I'm going to be married?"

"To whom?"

"Lizzie Mc-Swat. Are you going to marry?"

"Absolutely."

"Whom?"

"A man."

"A real man? How did he propose to you?"

"He didn't propose. He just stood up in the corner and said yes. I'd have strangled him if he had said no."

"What kind of a wife would you advise me to take?"

"Don't take a wife at all. Court the single women and leave the wives alone."

THE LOWRYS

"Don't you love Longfellow's poems?"

"Can't say I do. In fact, I have never read them. I consider all poetry absolute drivel."

"But surely you cannot help admiring this verse of his out of 'The Day Is Done':

"'And the night shall be filled with music,
    And the cares which infest the day
  Shall fold their tents like the Arabs
    And as silently steal away.'

"Now, isn't there truth in those few lines?"

"By Jove, there is something in that. I know those Arabs; they would steal anything."

———

"But say, I'll never go to dinner with you again."

"Why, what's the trouble now?"

"What's the trouble now? What did you say when the waiter brought you a plate of toothpicks? What did you do?"

"What did I do?"

"You know what you did. You said, 'No, thanks; I have already eaten three of the awful things, and I want no more.'"

"Neither did I want any more. They were awful things to eat."

"You shouldn't have eaten them. And another thing, why didn't you tip the waiter? Don't you know it's no more than right to give a waiter a liberal tip?"

"I gave the waiter more than a liberal tip; I gave him an immense tip."

"You did? Why, how much did you give him?"

"A nickel."

"My, but that was a large tip! I hope he doesn't get drunk with it."

"So do I."

"What made you give him such a large tip?"

"Didn't you see the fine hat and cane he picked out for me?"

JOE LAURIE AND ALEEN BRONSON

"Why, you impudent boy, I have a notion to slap you in the face."

"Let's go swimming."

"Let's go swimming? What's that got to do with it?"

"Didn't you say you had an ocean? Let's sail boats."

"Notion! Notion! Notion."

"I heard you, I heard you. If you don't want to swim, let's go wading."

"I said a notion."

"Oh, well, that's different. I take back my invitations."

"What do you do?"

"Who, me? I'm a census taker. If you have any left I'll be forced to take 'em."

"Well, you need 'em."

"My father is a millionaire."

"He is?"

"Yes, he is, and a rich one."

"Oh, look at that deck of cards I found in your coat. I'll bet you are a gambler."

"I suppose if you found a nickel in my vest you'd say I was a conductor."

"You're single, aren't you, girlie?"

"No, I have been married about a year."

"Oh, well, why didn't you say so? I gotta work different now."

GREEN ROOM CLUB DRESS REHEARSAL

The Green Room Club had a gala night recently at its Dress Rehearsal. Every now and then these chaps get together under the leadership of old John Peebles and assemble enough headliners to fit out forty vaudeville shows and put 'em all on in one night. Considerable night! Don't miss the next one.

Who did they have with them but His Obesity Irvin Cobb, who stood right up in front of everybody and told funny stories. That feller is ambidextrous, you know. He can use his tongue as well as his pen. Of course, he had to ring in his now historic interview with Lord Kitchener, but then no man is perfect, y' know.

After the buzz of admiration, which ran through the house at Cobb's entrance, had subsided, he began:

"I'm not a professional entertainer. I am only an amateur. I have been dragooned in here to do what I can to help along this benefit.

"It is now too late in the evening to hurt it badly. So I will venture to tell just one little darky story.

"Some of you doubtless remember that I went to Europe during the war in the interests of history, and when I was over there I interviewed Lord Kitchener.

"I have a friend down in Connecticut whose colored servant girl was very much interested in my articles. She painfully read them all with every evidence of the keenest interest in the great conflict.

"The morning after the Kitchener interview appeared she was in a state of great excitement when she came in to serve her master's breakfast.

"'This-all war,' she said, 'is gona last three years.'

"'It's going to last three years, is it, Miranda? How do you know it is going to last that long?'

"'De King of Europe told Ty Cobb so.'"

In response to the applause Cobb said:

"This, I suppose, is a curtain call, so I'll tell another story.

"A colored woman down in Greenville, S. C., married a darky who worked in the freight yards.

"About two weeks after the wedding ceremony the bridegroom was struck by a switch engine. He was of a fleshy disposition and the engine distributed him along the right of way in such a manner that he was a total loss.

"A claim agent for the railroad got wind of the accident and made a bee line for the widow before any other lawyer could outstrip him on his errand of mercy. It was just another of those cases in which the legal profession outdo each other in the effort to speed the wheels of justice.

"The claim agent had supplied himself with $500 in

crisp new bills, which he waved in front of the widow's face like a boy baiting a donkey with carrots. The colored woman didn't know there was that much money in the world. She reached for the bills with one hand and with the other hand she signed on the dotted line of the quit-claim.

"Another colored woman who had come along to help her friend bear up under the ordeal of grief remarked:

"'Clarissa, what do you reckon you're gona do, since you've had all this luck?'

"Before she answered, Clarissa took one of the twenty-dollar bills and thoughtfully inhaled its fragrance. Then she fanned herself with it and uttered a sigh of deep comfort and satisfaction.

"'First, Ah'm gona take a long rest and enjoy the comforts of this spending money. Dat's all I'll do jest for the present. It may be in years to come I may marry again—and I may not. Only time can tell. But, gal, I can tell you right now that if I ever do marry again, ma second husband is suttingly gona be a railroad man.'"

Ed Wynn as announcer for the other acts interpolated some of his own stuff. He came out with a rope tied to his left arm, by which, he explained, persons in the wings could pull him off and make room for the other acts.

"If anybody in the audience will name a subject," Wynn said, "I will endeavor to make a joke about it on the spur of the moment. Just any subject whatever. I will show my great dexterity of mind by immediately creating a funny joke on that subject. Do I hear any suggestions?"

"Soap," shouted somebody in the audience.

"Somebody has suggested 'soap,'" Wynn said. "Very well. Here goes. They say they have captured Villa. They captured him on Easter Sunday. Where was he? He was in a church.

"How did they know he was in a church?

"The bell tol'd."

Great laughter by the audience as persons tried to figure where the soap connection came in.

"Now anybody else name a subject. I want to demonstrate again how easily I make up jokes on any given subject without a moment's previous notice."

Some one in the audience suggested "matches."

"Matches. All right," said Wynn. "A lady went into a restaurant and ordered fish. When the waiter brought the fish she tasted it and didn't like it. She said to the waiter, 'This fish isn't good. I expect to get good fish here. Take this fish to the proprietor and tell him I complained of it because it was bad. A week ago I had some fish here and it was excellent.'

"'Why, you're crazy,' said the waiter, 'this is a piece of the same fish.'"

Then they pulled Wynn off with the rope.

Elizabeth Murray told this one:

"The Ancient Order of Hibernians was getting ready for its Saint Patrick's Day parade. The old Irishman in charge of the parade plans said:

"'Now I want all you straight-backed, broad-shouldered, fine built men to form in the first ranks of the parade.

"'Then in the rear ranks I want all you old bow-legged, hump-backed fellows.

"'Now I'll tell you why I want all the straight-backed, square-shouldered marchers in the foremost division.

"'It is so that when we pass by the reviewing stand, the A. P. A.'s in the crowd can't say we were crooked from the start!'"

McWATERS AND TYSON

"Poor Jones, did you hear about him?"

"No."

"Lots of trouble. First his business went."

"Too bad."

"Then his house went."

"O, wasn't that unfortunate?"

"Then his wife went, and at last his automobile went."

"Great! It's the first time in years! It never went before."

CROSS (IN A MONOLOGUE)

Once I addressed the prisoners in a state penitentiary. I occupied the platform for about twenty minutes telling the convicts a number of humorous stories and jokes. When I finished there was handclapping, and when I left the platform a grizzled old life timer who had been in twenty-five years already came up to me.

"I want to shake your hand," he said. "I can't tell you how much I enjoyed hearing all the old jokes again."

That reminds me of Henry Ford. Lots of people laugh at him, but he did what he thought was right and spent his money trying to stop the war. I think he ought to be given some recognition.

I had thought of having all the 4d cars stop at a certain time on a certain day—but then they might never get them started again.

I drove one myself all summer. It didn't have a speedometer, but I could tell when it was going twelve miles an hour by the way my teeth chattered.

JAMES DIAMOND AND SYBIL BRENNAN

"You are the girl of my dreams."

"Aren't you nice and gallant?"

"I have had some awful dreams lately."

"My mother was an actress, and I could have been an actress for nothing."

"My father was a minister, and I could have been good for nothing."

"O, you make me tired with your nonsense. Men don't know anything, anyway. It's the women that know things."

"I know it; that's why we stay out late at night."

"What do you mean?"

"Gosh, we've got to learn something."

"You keep on staying out nights and you'll never go to heaven."

"I don't care; I own the other place."

"You own it?"

"Yes, my wife gave it to me this morning."

"Kiss me."

"Mother won't like it."

"Mother isn't going to get it."

"Don't you know that kissing spreads contagion?"

"Poison me at once, because, darling, I love you."

"You have loved me a long while?"

"Yes, sweetheart; I have loved you and your sister. And I have dreamed that maybe some day you would become my wife, and we could move into a nice flat, and take your sister as a boarder."

GEORGE ARMSTRONG

I often heard about how good a Philadelphia lawyer is, but I don't think they have anything on me.

Last month Bill Johnson brought me up on a charge of breaking into his hen house. I fought the case all my own self. I told the judge I didn't break into it at all. I said: "I found one of the windows of the hen house open and I merely inserted my right arm and removed a few trifling hens from their perch." Now, of course, anybody knows my arm is not myself, and I told the judge just what I thought about it, and I fail to see how any one can punish the individual for an offense committed only by one of his limbs.

"That argument," said the judge to me, "is indeed very well put up. Following it logically I sentence the man's arm to one year imprisonment. He can accompany it or not, just as he chooses."

With a smile I unscrewed my cork arm, left it with the judge, and walked out.

"I was up in the Manicure club the other night."

"What is the Manicure club? What do you do there?"

"We sit up all night trying to better each other's hands."

"How do you figure it that a man who wins at cards nearly always loses on the horses?"

"Well, you can't shuffle horses."

EMMA CARUS AND LARRY COMER

"You have grown thinner since last season, haven't you?"

"Yes, about eighty pounds."

"Does it seem to make any difference?"

"Well, I should remark! The American people are

beginning to gaze with pleasure on anything that has been reduced."

" Really, how many times have you been married? "

" Fifty-five, not counting my last husband."

"What is your idea in marrying so many times? "

"Some time I may get a good one."

"Well, why is it that love cannot go on forever? "

" The chief reason is that people insist on getting married."

LEONA THURBER AND HARRY MADISON

" I have a terrible cold. I was visiting a friend the other night, and she served some draft beer."

" But how did you get your cold? "

" I sat in the draft."

" Have you any nice fresh farmer's eggs? "

"No, only hen's."

" What is butter today? "

" Same as it was yesterday—butter."

"Fresh. And what are prunes? "

" Prunes are raisins with inflammatory rheumatism."

WELLINGTON CROSS AND
LOIS JOSEPHINE

"Weren't you at the fair in San Francisco?"

"Yes, I was."

"I knew it. I was sure I had seen you there. You stayed at the Palatial hotel, didn't you? Ah, I remember it all now. Yes, I stayed there all summer and I remember seeing you almost every day."

"That's odd."

"Why so?"

"Because I spent the summer in Maine."

ARCHIE NICHOLSON

I'll never forget the time I first got married. It was on Friday, the 13th, 1913. No wonder I call Fridays and the number thirteen unlucky.

The first meal she cooked was a pie, but the flour was so tough I could hardly cut it. I had to blame it on the flour, 'cause she's a big, strong woman, and I believe in safety first. But still, Rose is so gentle! Yes, her name is Rose; but, believe me, that's the first rose I ever saw without a scent. She ain't got no money.

Still, she wanted a piano right away, so I had to buy one for her. I paid $500.65 for it—$3 down and a dollar when they catch me in. And more yet besides, I didn't even get trading stamps with it.

But, believe me, my wife she certainly can sing. Last night she sang "William Tell." But I stood out on the street, by the door, so the neighbors could see I wasn't hurting her.

JOHN B. HYMER AND COMPANY

Mr. Hymer (debating whether he should give his savings to the stranded actress so she will be able to reach the bedside of her dying baby) —Now afore I gib dis money away I muss talk it ovah wif my soul. Soul, muss I gib dis money to de lady or muss I keep it? (Sotto voce: Gib it to her; gib it all to her.) Now, listen, soul, jess a minnit, less us getting together on dis thing. Ah's goin' to ax yuh agin, now you th'nk it ovah, muss I gib dis money to de lady or muss I keep it? (Sotto voce: Gib it to her, gib it all to her.) Now, soul, jess a minnit, hab you taken all things into consideration? **Don't go and do** nuffin rash. Be calm and collected, muss I **gib** it all to her? Ah'll haf tu get a lot moah ob my unknown percentage on dis job ef I do. (Sotto voce: Gib it all to her.) Soul, you win. I wouldn't **nevvah** be satumfied till it am all gone, anyhow.

CAITS BROTHERS

" I can't work without any light; that's all there is to it. Hey, spotlight, man — give me some light."

" How much do you weigh? "

" Ninety - eight pounds."

" You're light enough."

C. E. EVANS AND HELENA PHILLIPS

" Did you see anything of my razor? "

" Yes, it is over there on the dressing table. I used it to sharpen my pencil this morning."

" What is the second number in the combination to this safe? "

" Is the second number necessary? "

NAT GOODWIN IN MONOLOGUE

The other day some friends were talking with my wife—that is, my present wife—about the wedding of Geraldine Farrar. When Miss Farrar was married to Lou Tellegen she had the event photographed on a film. And she had the voices of the guests recorded on phonograph records. In later years she will be able to show this wedding on the screen in her private home for the benefit of intimate friends, thus providing half an hour's unusual entertainment.

"Gee," I said, "why didn't I think of that?" If I had had my marriages filmed I could have provided not only one episode, but a big moving picture serial. A great program, and, like all theatrical programs, subject to change without notice.

One day the census taker came to my little home in Santa Barbara, Cal. He asked me the usual questions —my name, did I own my house, was it mortgaged? Then he inquired: "Are you single, married, or divorced?" I told him, "Yes."

At the Garrick Club in London I found myself talking with an English actor of the thick, impervious type, and after he had learned that I was supposed to be a comedian he asked me to give a sample of American humor so he could judge for himself if American humor was as flat and senseless as it was reported to be. I told him he wouldn't like our stuff and begged to be excused, but with British persistency he hung on until I told him this story:

A stranger got off the train in a small Pennsylvania town one foggy day and asked the first native he met: "Do you know where the postoffice is?"

The native said, "Yes," and walked right by.

The stranger started on, and the native came back, laughed apologetically and explained:

"I was merely trying to have a little fun. But do you really want to know where the postoffice is?"

And the stranger said, "No."

When the Englishman was informed that that was the end of the story, he exclaimed:

"I think they were both jolly rude, that's what I think of them."

I was stopping at a hotel in Denver and had to catch a 5 o'clock train for Leadville the next morning. The night watchman was a jolly Irishman, and he assured me that he himself would wake me up in plenty of time. "Don't worry the clerk or the bellboy," he said: "I'll call ye myself." I crawled into bed, dead tired, and it seemed that about five minutes had elapsed when I heard a rough knock at my door and the voice of the watchman call out: "Are you the man that was to catch a 5 o'clock train? Well, go back to sleep, it's now 6 o'clock, and your train's gone an hour ago."

Some years ago I was playing in a serious piece called "Nathan Hale," and I had the role of Hale, who, as you know, was hanged by the British. One night I gave a pair of tickets to my friend Charley Hoyt, now dead—and a wittier, jollier fellow never lived. At the last moment Mrs. Hoyt couldn't come, so Charley went along Broadway trying to find some one to give the ticket to. Finally he found a fellow who had no engagement that evening, but he refused to accept the ticket and accompany Hoyt to see me.

"Why not?" asked Hoyt.

"Because I don't like that fellow Goodwin."

"Come on, then," declared Hoyt, "you'll have a lovely evening. They hang him in the last act."

I used to know an old fellow named Gray, who had an impediment in his speech. One day he touched my arm at the club and said:

"H-a-a-ave you g-g-g-got h-h-h-half an hour to s-s-spare? I want to have five minutes' conversation with you."

The same old fellow took me with him one day when he went to a dog fancier to buy a rat terrier. He said he would pay a good price, but he wanted to be sure he got a dog that would actually go after the rats. The dog man finally sold my friend a little green-colored terrier for $400.

"You've got a good dog cheap," the man said, "for the way that dog pulverizes rats is a caution."

So they put the dog in the rat pit to show him off. They brought in a big gray rat that looked about as long as this walking stick. The rat sort of crouched beside the wall and the terrier stood and blinked at him in a stupid, friendly manner. The rat gave a leap and set his teeth through the dog's upper lip. The terrier let out a wail, shook the rat off, jumped over the railing and tore out down Broadway howling like a steam calliope going by on a racing car. My friend who had bought the dog turned and gave the seller a funny look and asked:

"H-h-how much will you t-t-take for the rat?"

A comedian arose from an all-night poker game and went out into the world dead broke and with a tremendous thirst. An idea struck him. He went into a cafe and ordered a silver gin fizz. While the bar-tender was mixing it, the actor began telling funny stories. The bartender laughed, and the funnier the stories got, the louder the barkeep laughed. The actor finished his fizz and started out.

"Did you pay me for that?" the bartender asked.

"Sure, I paid you after the third story. You were laughing so that you don't remember it."

When the actor had gone half a block he met another comedian, also broke and thirsty. He told the second man to go right down to the cafe on the corner and tell the bartender funny stories. He went in and asked:

"Do you like funny stories?"

The bartender replied: "I did once, but I'm cured."

The man ordered a silver gin fizz and began telling comic tales. By the time he had recounted three the bartender was smiling in spite of himself. At the sixth story the bartender was laughing aloud.

"Cut out this funny business," he said. "A chap was in here a while ago telling funny stories, and I don't know whether he paid for his drink or not."

The second comedian said: "Never mind about that other fellow; you give me my change."

BONITA AND LEW HEARN

"Do you ever have shows in your town, sheriff?"

"Yep, we had a show there a long time ago. They called it 'South Boston.' It was an awful sad piece."

"South Boston!"

"I think that was it."

"O, it must have been 'East Lynn.'"

"Durned if I don't think you're right. I knew it was some town in Massachusetts."

"And so you've been married?"

"Yes, my first wife died early."

"What was the trouble?"

"She sat down on a tack and she was so short it pierced her heart."

"O, how unfortunate!"

"Yes, and I had another misfortune the other day. My wife and I were reading when some one threw a bomb through the window and it exploded in the room. My wife and I were blown through the window at the same time."

"Is it possible?"

"Yes; that was the first time the wife and I had been out together in eight years."

"How old is this wine, waiter?"

"Twenty years."

"It's awfully small for its age. How much does it cost?"

"Five dollars."

"How much?"

"Ten dollars."

"I heard you the first time."

CLARK AND HAMILTON

" Haven't we met before? "

" I believe not."

" I think I met you at a reception. It was in the conservatory."

" Conservatory? "

" Yes. Don't you understand? The garden."

" Garden? "

" Yes, the shrubbery, the shrubbery, out near the alley."

" No, I don't recall you."

" But I have seen you somewhere. It may have been during the hunting season."

" Hunting season? "

" Yes, I was one of the hounds."

" Were you ever presented at court? "

" Yes, every Monday morning."

" I'd like some lunch."

" I'd like to see you get it."

" Don't be flip with me; I'm a lady."

" Never mind, I'll never betray your secret."

"ABE POTASH"
(By Montague Glass)

" In business a man couldn't be too careful about the friends he is making," said Abe Potash, when interviewed at the theatre by a representative of the Daily Cloak and Suit Gazette, " because it is an old saying and a true one that competition makes a spicy life. If you make friends out of your competitors it gets to be too spicy, and don't you forget it!

"As soon as you make a friend of a competitor he would drop in at your flat every time you are entertaining an important customer, and not only would he eat your food on you, but if you play pinochle after dinner he would on purpose lose four hundred hands by two points, so that he could show what a helluva good loser he is before your customer. Leon Sammett copped out two accounts on me that way, and now if I've got up to five hundred on forty jacks and sixty queens, I never let anyone get the bid away from me when I am playing with a customer in the game. You can take it from me, a competitor couldn't be a friend even on Sundays or legal holidays.

"From a customer also you should be careful about making a friend, because when you sell goods to a friend he thinks you are trying to stick him, and you think he ain't going to pay you, and usually you are both right. Also, again, the more friends you've got among your customers the more postage stamps you buy for mailing monthly statements, because, as my partner, Mawruss Perlmutter, always says, 'old friends is always the slowest.' A merchant who prides himself that he makes a personal friend out of a customer should get a rubber stamp made:

THIS ACCOUNT IS OVERDUE
PLEASE REMIT

He could save himself writer's cramp that way.

"Once more, also, you should be particular about making a friend from the feller you buy goods off. Lots of ladies is going around in garments Mawruss and me manufactured which cost $5 for workmanship, $10 for material and fifty cents on account of some filet mignon which Louis Mintz, the salesman of the Hamswickett Mills, blew us to and added to the cost of the piece goods when he billed them to us. Louis is such a good friend of us that we couldn't kick about it so we don't buy from him any more.

"No one returns goods on you so much as friends. In particular, I had a friend by the name of Harris Fashman, who shipped us back a $75 dinner gown which had a pint of lockshum soup spilled all down the front panel, and when we refused to accept it he got awful sore, and said, 'Didn't we expect that his wife must eat like the same as anybody else?'

"When you make a friend from a customer you should be sure to get from him a signed statement of his assets, otherwise you would sooner or later got to settle with him for ten cents on the dollar, because a shaky retailer's best friend always shows up strong in his list of creditors. His enemies made his life so miserable that he paid 'em all up months before he filed his petition in bankruptcy.

"Furthermore, if you allow a customer to become your friend, he would take advantage from you in other ways. A customer of ours by the name of Charles Schuldenfrei of Bridgeport was in our store last month and he made such a hog with himself with some lobster a la Newburg which Mawruss bought for him for supper after the theatre that when he went to bed he got an idea he was dying. In the middle of the night he sent out for a stomach specialist at $20 a call and he told him to mail the bill to us. As he, Schuldenfrei, already owed us $850, we couldn't let an account like that die on us. I told Mawruss that the next time he entertains Schuldenfrei, the last thing before seeing him to the hotel, he should buy Schuldenfrei for five cents a drink of bicarbonate of soda and leave him the telephone number of a reasonable general practitioner like Dr. Eichendorfer. If you act so easy with such a feller as Schuldenfrei, the first thing you know he would be getting appendicitis on you and expecting him to blow you to an emergency operation, with two trained nurses and a private room in Mount Sinai Hospital.

"After all, a man's best friend is his partner, and even a partner you shouldn't be too friendly with neither. It's an old saying, 'Familiarity is a dangerous thing,' and if you want your partner to respect you, you shouldn't be so friendly with him that you couldn't once in a while call him all kinds of names."

FORRESTER AND LLOYD

"Well, we're back home again."

"Yes; and we saw some fine sights."

"You said it. Wasn't the Delaware river beautiful?"

"It sure was."

"Right where we were standing George Washington crossed it in a rowboat."

"Yes, I know he did; but I don't see why he went to all that trouble of rowing across the river when he could have saved himself a lot of work."

"I don't understand. What do you mean?"

"Well, why didn't George wait until the river froze and then skate across?"

"By the way you talk it is easily seen that you don't come from the social set."

"Don't say that. My relatives have been wonders."

"You don't say?"

"Yes; and my grandfather figured in one of Thackeray's novels."

"How is that?"

"Do you remember that passage where it says, 'Waiter, rack punch?'"

"I believe I do remember that passage."

"Well, my grandfather was that waiter."

———

THE HENNINGS

"See that wagon over there?"

"Certainly. Why doesn't it move?"

"The wheels are tired."

———

ANTHONY AND MACK

"I'm going to help a rich bricklayer get up into society. He just got a few hundred thousand left to him. I've been waiting half an hour for him and he hasn't showed up yet. Probably he got acquainted with a real estate lawyer and invested his money in bum property."

(Mack enters.) (Anthony continues):

"Where have you been so long?"

"Sure, Oi met an old friend."

"Yes, and I suppose you have been patronizing every saloon on the avenue?"

" No, not every ; only the ones me old man used to
own."

" So your father used to own saloons? "

" Sure."

" And tell me, how many did he own on the avenue? "

" Well, Oi'll tell yer, I always thought he owned five
until Oi just met me friend. Now Oi know he owned
seventy-five."

" By the way, I haven't learned your name yet."

" Me name? "

" Yes, and soon as we get acquainted I'll teach you
how to get up in society."

" Foist teach me how ter get up in the mornin'."

" Well, are you going to tell me your name? "

" Sure, it's Irving Mack."

" Irving Mack? Well, then, Irving Mack, what was
your father's name? "

" Irving."

" His last name."

" Sure, it's the same as mine."

COLEMAN

The town I was in last week was a very amusing
town, indeed. It had a great many stores, so I amused
myself by inspecting the different shop windows.

While I was admiring some ties in a large department store window I was considering whether I should
speculate in a tie or a bottle of rum. A little boy came
out of this large store, looked up at me, hesitated a
minute and finally caught me by the sleeve. Well,
anyhow, the boy took hold of me by the sleeve and said,

"Please, mister, will you come into this store with me?"

"Certainly," answered I.

I followed him into the store. At the counter the little fellow astonished me and every one else who was standing around by remarking: "There, miss, mother wants the ribbon the same color as this man's nose."

ARCHER AND BELFORD

He—What's this? A pass to get a drink?

She—Of course not. I wish you would oblige us by voting this ticket.

"What kind of a ticket is it?"

"Open it and read it, then you will see for yourself."

"But, lady, I can't read a word."

"You can't read a word?"

"That's what I said, lady."

"Well, then, I will explain it to you. This ballot means that you are willing to let the women vote as well as the men."

"Is that what it says?"

"Yes, sir."

"Then I don't want it."

"And pray, tell me why you won't vote it?"

"'Cause the women don't know enough to vote."

"What kind of a specimen are you? You can't read, still you have an idea that you're brighter than the women. In fact, you can't do anything."

"Oh, yes, I can, lady. I can drink more booze than any man in my line of business."

"What I mean is you have no profession."

"I ain't got no profession, but I've got a great appetite."

"You still don't understand. What I mean is, you have no skill with your hands."

"Yes, I have, lady. My hands are trained to pick up any amount of money folks drop."

"No, no; what I mean is, you can't do anything such as writing or painting."

"I can draw good."

"What did you ever draw?"

"Last night I drew six aces in a poker game."

"I mean artistic drawing."

"I think it's pretty artistic work to be able to draw six aces in one game."

Case's New Book of
CONUNDRUMS AND RIDDLES
By Carleton B. Case

160 Pages   **Paper Covers**   **Price 40 Cents**

Our young folks can have a host of fun with this Conundrum Book in the home,—and the older folks, too. Some of these Riddles are brand new, and all of them are good, being selected as the very choicest from the wits of all nations and every age. The answer is given to every one of the Conundrums—except that those on the first page are a play upon the names of people whom you know, and require no answers. When you get the book, try some of the Conundrums without reading the answers; then spring them on your friends.

SHREWESBURY PUBLISHING CO.
5311 West Lake Street, CHICAGO

FLASHES OF IRISH WIT

By Carleton B. Case

160 Pages   **Paper Covers**   **Price 40 Cents**

The best bulls, blunders and banter by the sons and daughters of the Emerald Isle, gathered into one volume for the delectation of all who appreciate a hearty laugh. This is not a mere collection from the ancient Irish authors, with their ''Handy Andys'' and other butts and jokers, but, in the main, is the best wit of the modern, the transplanted Irishman, the kind that Americans best know and appreciate. You will agree, when you peruse it, that it is the most mirth-provoking collection of real good Irish fun you never read, and to say that is equivalent to saying that it is a book of unsurpassed humor, for the Irishman above all others ''takes the cake'' as a natural wit.

SHREWESBURY PUBLISHING CO.
5311 West Lake Street, CHICAGO

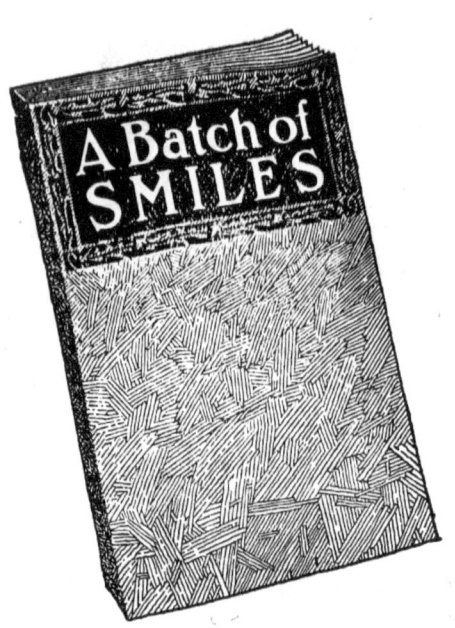

A BATCH OF SMILES

By Carleton B. Case

160 Pages   **Paper Covers**   **Price 40 Cents**

A collection of the most laughable jokes, doings and sayings of funny folks, gathered from every quarter of the globe; warranted to produce a smile on the longest face. Comprising original and selected anecdotes by the world's best wits, some of which have never before been in print, and all of them funny and laugh-provoking; such humor as ladies and gentlemen appreciate, and are better and happier for the having. This little book of clean fun has carried happiness all around the world, as we have had orders for copies from Asia, Africa and the isles of the seven seas.

SHREWESBURY PUBLISHING CO.

5311 West Lake Street, CHICAGO

THE SUNNY SIDE OF LIFE
By Carleton B. Case

160 Pages **Paper Covers** **Price 40 Cents**

The felicitous and witty sayings and doings of people that start us all to smiling and furnish us with hearty amusement. Short bits of real humor selected from the world's newest and best,—clean and wholesome, suitable for the family circle and all who appreciate a good laugh. A book to be enjoyed and passed on to appreciative friends, that the smiles may go 'round and all be the happier for a brief glimpse of the sunny side of life. The merry quip and the happily turned anecdote always will hold the human interest. This collection is a splendid exponent of the best in wholesome fun.

SHREWESBURY PUBLISHING CO.
5311 West Lake Street, CHICAGO

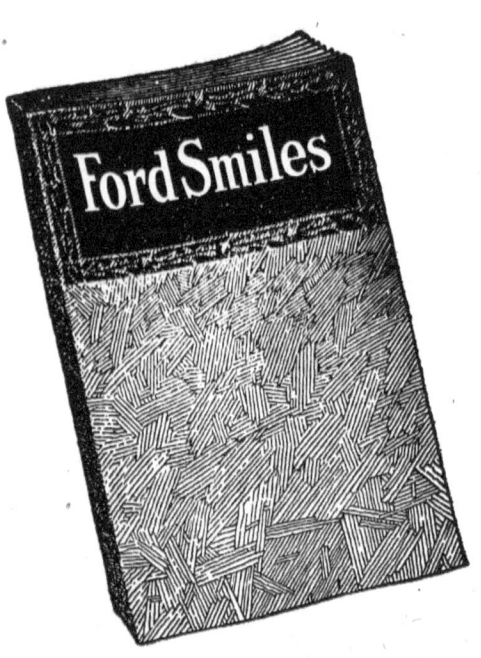

FORD SMILES

By Carleton B. Case

160 Pages   **Paper Covers**   **Price 40 Cents**

The very newest, largest and choicest collection of merry quips about our friend the Ford car, all good natured and laughable, with nothing to offend even Ma Henry Ford himself. The author went to Detroit and obtained some of the new jokes in this book right at the Ford factory. You can't help laughing, whether you own a Ford car or not, at the funny things in "Ford Smiles." When you get this book of humor we ask you to read the short Preface to it; it explains, in the author's opinion, why every good Ford joke is a compliment to that great invention—the Ford Motor Car. Probably you hadn't thought of it that way.

SHREWESBURY PUBLISHING CO.
5311 West Lake Street, CHICAGO

BLACK-FACE FUN and MINSTREL GUIDE

By Carleton B. Case

160 Pages　　　**Paper Covers**　　　**Price 40 Cents**

There is more fun in a good home minstrel show than in any other you can give. This book tells you just how to go about it to put a black-face show on and over successfully and profitably. And besides that, it is one of the funniest books to read, being full of the best minstrel and negro jokes, monologues, retorts, gags, cross-fire talk, catches and stump speeches. This is the newest and most complete work of its kind, full of hearty laughs, and a joy to all, young and not so young. Worth many times its price, as you'll agree when you read it.

SHREWESBURY PUBLISHING CO.
5311 West Lake Street, CHICAGO

GOOD STORIES ABOUT ROOSEVELT
BY CARLETON B. CASE

160 Pages   **Paper Covers**   **Price 40 Cents**

The humorous side of this great American. Anecdotes of his boyhood, college days, ranch life, hunting and exploring trips; as a Rough Rider; during his extended political life in New York, Albany and Washington, as Assemblyman, Police Commissioner, Governor, Assistant Secretary of the Navy, Vice-President and President, and in his retirement. No other great man since Lincoln has seen the humorous aspect of life in all its phases as did Roosevelt. The fun he found in all places and under all circumstances makes a bookful of laughter for your entertainment. None is too old and few too young to enjoy it.

SHREWESBURY PUBLISHING CO.
5311 West Lake Street, CHICAGO

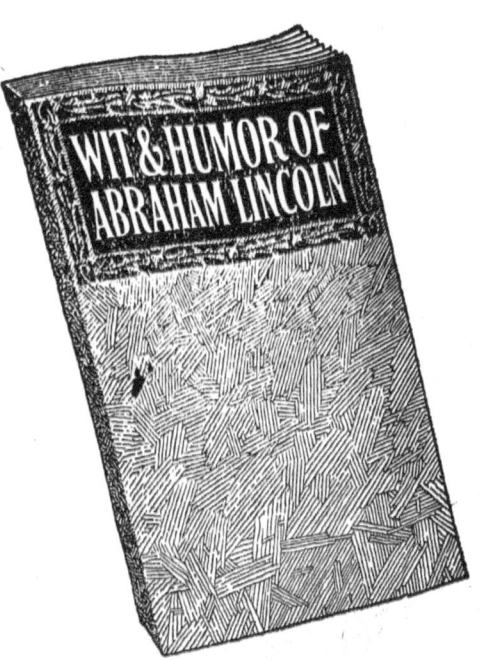

THE SHREWESBURY SERIES OF
Popular Entertainment Books
In Attractive Paper Covers

Edited by CARLETON B. CASE

The very latest works of their kind. Uniform in style. Procurable where you bought this book, or will be sent postpaid by the publishers on receipt of price.

SHREWESBURY PUBLISHING CO.

5311 West Lake Street, CHICAGO

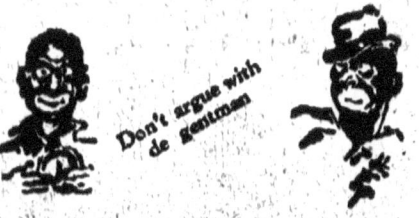